Oxford English ⠀⠀⠀⠀⠀⠀⠀⠀...onary

Diccionario Oxford
de Inglés Ilustrado

E C PARNWELL

ilustrado por
Corinne Clarke y Ray Burrows

Sociedad General Española de Librería
Oxford University Press

COMO USAR ESTE DICCIONARIO ILUSTRADO

Para encontrar el equivalente de la palabra en inglés de algo que está buscando, fíjese en el índice general. En el índice hallará el número de la página ilustrada que le mostrará la palabra que busca. Todos los objetos los encontrará en sus grupos naturales, por ejemplo: todos los animales los encontrará en la página encabezada **Animales** o en la página encabezada **En la granja.** Cuando mire las ilustraciones podrá observar que junto a todos los animales se han colocado números. Observe los números debajo de cada ilustración y junto a ellos encontrará los nombres ingleses correspondientes.

Una vez que haya encontrado la palabra que buscaba, trate de aprender al mismo tiempo algunas otras palabras que se encuentran en la misma página. Cubra todas las palabras y haga la prueba de ver cuántas de ellas puede recordar.

En el índice que comienza en la página 81 encontrará una lista de todas las palabras inglesas en orden alfabético. Junto a estas palabras hay un símbolo fonético con el objeto de que el lector pueda aprender a pronunciarlas también y además las palabras tienen dos números: por ejemplo **26/3**. El primer número le indica en qué página se encuentra el objeto y el segundo le dice a qué objeto se refiere la palabra.

© *Oxford University Press 1977*
Ninth impression 1993
ISBN 0 19 431202 X

Printed in Hong Kong

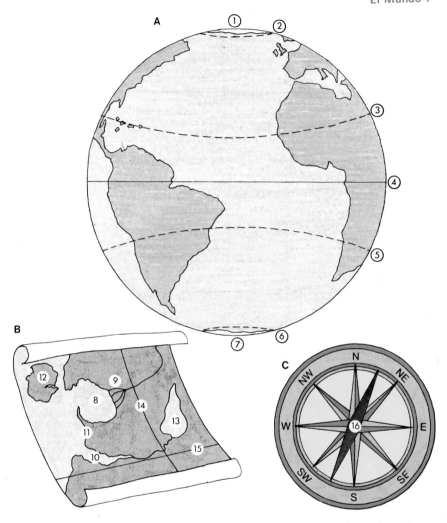

A. **Globo**
1 Polo Norte
2 Círculo Artico
3 Trópico de Cáncer
4 Ecuador
5 Trópico de Capricornio
6 Círculo Antártico
7 Polo Sur

B. **Mapa**
8 bahía
9 delta
10 estuario
11 costa
12 isla

13 lago
14 longitud
15 latitud

C. **Brújula**
16 aguja
N   norte
NE noreste
E   este
SE sureste
S   sur
SW suroeste
W   oeste
NW noroeste

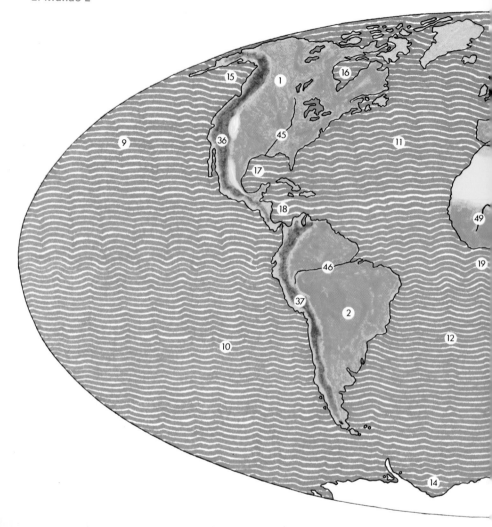

A.	Continentes		C.	Mares, Golfos, Bahías
1	América del Norte		15	Golfo de Alaska
2	América del Sur		16	Bahía de Hudson
3	Europa		17	Golfo de Méjico
4	Africa		18	Mar Caribe
5	Asia		19	Golfo de Guinea
6	Australia		20	Mar del Norte
7	Antártida		21	Mar Báltico
			22	Mar Mediterráneo
B.	Océanos		23	Mar Negro
8	Artico		24	Mar Caspio
9	Pacífico del Norte		25	Mar Rojo
10	Pacífico del Sur		26	Golfo Pérsico
11	Atlántico del Norte		27	Mar de Arabia
12	Atlántico del Sur		28	Golfo de Bengala
13	Indico		29	Mar del Coral
14	Meridional		30	Mar de Tasmania

1	camisa	**13**	sombrero
2	cuello	**14**	abrigo
3	puño	**15**	solapa
4	corbata	**16**	bolsillo
5	chaleco	**17**	pantalones
6	traje	**18**	vuelta
7	manga	**19**	bufanda
8	zapato	**20**	guante
9	cordón	**21**	reloj
10	suela	**22**	correa de reloj
11	tacón	**23**	gafas
12	impermeable	**24**	paraguas, sombrilla

1 sostén	**11** collar
2 combinación/enaguas	**12** lima de uñas
3 bragas	**13** polvera
4 medias	**14** pestañina/rimel
5 chal/mantilla	**15** esmalte de uñas
6 camisón	**16** perfume/esencia
	17 sombra de ojos
7 zapatilla	**18** crema para la cara
8 anillo	**19** lápiz de labios
9 pulsera	
10 pendiente	

1	blusa	**9**	abrigo
2	falda	**10**	cinturón
3	calcetín	**11**	hebilla
4	gorra	**12**	zapato
5	suéter/jersey	**13**	pañuelo
		14	pañuelo de bolsillo
6	pantalones	**15**	broche
7	sandalia	**16**	bolso
8	vestido	**17**	paraguas

1 buzón
2 paso de peatones
3 puesto de mercado
4 carretilla
5 taxi
6 bicicleta
7 semáforo
8 poste de señales   m
9 bordillo de acera

10 cuneta de calle
11 alcantarilla
12 parque
13 puente
14 camioneta
15 camión
16 cruce de carreteras
17 motocicleta
18 cochecito para niños

19	bloque de apartamentos	**28**	parada de autobús
20	bloque de oficinas	**29**	acera
21	anuncio	**30**	papelera
22	tienda	**31**	cabina telefónica
23	escaparate		
24	poste de la luz	**32**	estacionamiento
25	parquímetro	**33**	coche
26	autobús	**34**	carretera/calle
27	cobrador		

A. **Detención**
1   policía
2   casco
3   uniforme
4   comisaría
5   coche de policía
6   perro policía
7   porra
8   esposas
9   linterna
10 lupa
11 huellas digitales
12 huellas

B. **Cárcel/Prisión**
13 guardián
14 prisionero
15 celda
16 barras

C. **Corte de Justicia**
17 jurado
18 banquillo de los testigo
19 testigo
20 defendido/acusado
21 banquillo
22 juez
23 abogado
24 toga
25 peluca

1	grúa	14	trabajador
2	albañil	15	arena
3	viga	16	cemento
4	tejas	17	llana
5	escalera	18	artesa
6	escalón	19	azadón
7	andamio	20	excavadora
8	ladrillos	21	mezcladora de
9	tubería de desagüe		cemento/hormigón
10	cimientos	22	volquete
11	tablón	23	taladro neumático
12	pico/zapapico	24	cucharón
13	pala		

1 banco de trabajo	**9** pala
2 lima	**10** horquilla de jardín
3 papel de lija	**11** tijeras de jardín
4 cincel	**12** paleta
5 navaja/cuchillo	**13** llave
6 llave inglesa	**14** tenazas
7 destornillador	**15** hacha
8 torno de banco	

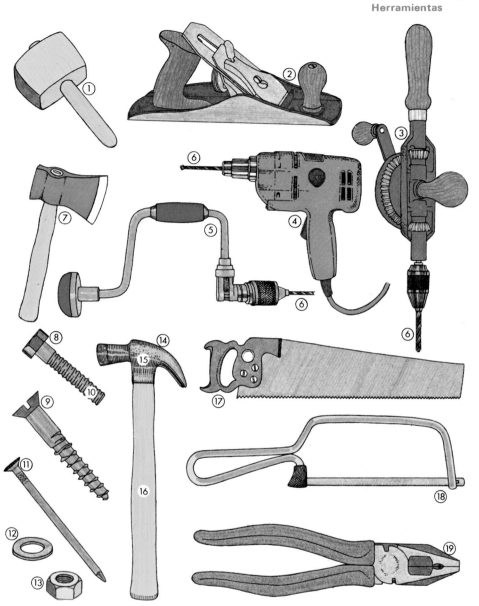

1 mazo	**11** clavo
2 cepillo de carpintero	**12** arandela
3 taladradora	**13** tuerca
4 taladradora eléctrica	**14** martillo
5 berbiquí	**15** cabeza
6 barrena	**16** mango
7 hacha	**17** serrucho
8 perno	**18** sierra para metales
9 tornillo	**19** alicates
10 rosca	

English		Spanish			Spanish
roof	1	tejado		12	contraventana
chimney	2	chimenea		13	jardinera
wall	3	pared		14	cortina
balcony	4	balcón		15	persiana
patio	5	patio		16	canalón
garage	6	garage		17	desagüe
(front) door	7	puerta		18	felpudo
window	8	ventana		19	antena
window-frame	9	marco		20	cobertizo
window-pane	10	vidrio		21	hierba
(window-)ledge/sill	11	alféizar			

El Tiempo		**14**	ramitas
1	relámpago o rayo	**15**	hojas
2	(tormenta) (trueno	**16**	puerta
	nube de	**17**	seto
3	lluvia	**18**	senda
4	gotas de lluvia	**19**	césped
5	nieve	**20**	flor
6	bola de nieve	**21**	macizo de flores
7	muñeco de nieve	**22**	arbusto/matorral
8	carámbano	**23**	regadera
9	sol	**24**	maceta
10	cielo	**25**	horquilla de jardín
		26	cobertizo
En el Jardín		**27**	carretilla
11	árbol	**28**	cuerda para tender la ropa
12	tronco	**29**	lavado
13	rama	**30**	pinzas para la ropa

ramo (handwritten annotation next to item 21)

1	puerta	**16**	peldaño
2	aldaba	**17**	escalera
3	timbre	**18**	barandilla
4	umbral	**19**	pasamanos
5	buzón	**20**	planta alta
6	ojo de la cerradura	**21**	planta baja
7	cerrojo y cadena	**22**	luz
8	cerrojo	**23**	interruptor
9	bisagra	**24**	reloj
10	felpudo	**25**	teléfono
11	suelo	**26**	auricular
12	alfombrilla	**27**	disco/marcador
13	perchero	**28**	cordón
14	percha	**29**	guía telefónica
15	llave		

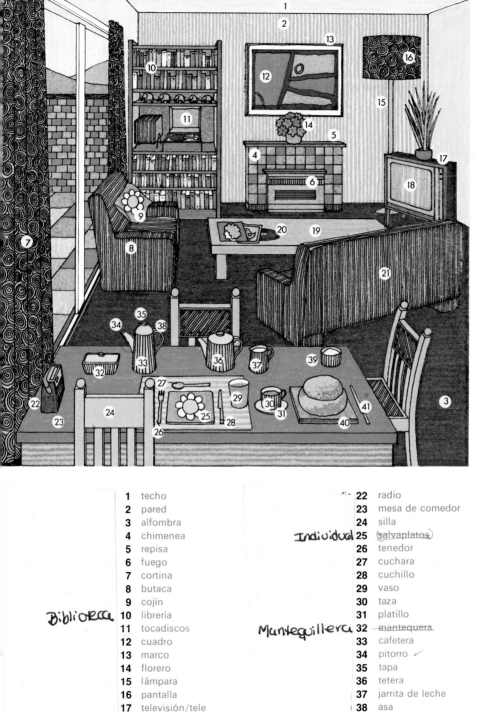

1	techo	22	radio
2	pared	23	mesa de comedor
3	alfombra	24	silla
4	chimenea	25	~~salvaplatos~~ *Individual*
5	repisa	26	tenedor
6	fuego	27	cuchara
7	cortina	28	cuchillo
8	butaca	29	vaso
9	cojin	30	taza
10	libreria *Biblioteca*	31	platillo
11	tocadiscos	32	~~mantequera~~ *Muntequillera*
12	cuadro	33	cafetera
13	marco	34	pitorro
14	florero	35	tapa
15	lámpara	36	tetera
16	pantalla	37	jarrita de leche
17	televisión/tele	38	asa
18	pantalla (de televisión)	39	azucarera
19	mesa ~~(de café)~~	40	tablero
20	disco	41	cuchillo
21	sofá/canapé		

1 cocina	**18** rodillo de repostero
2 horno	**19** lata para pasteles
3 parrilla	**20** jarra
4 placa	**21** abrelatas
5 refrigerador/nevera	**22** lata
6 despensa	**23** cesta
7 pila	**24** libro de cocina
8 desaguadero	**25** coiador
9 basura/cubo de basura	**26** rascador
10 estantería de verduras	**27** cepillo para lavar la vajill.
11 sartén	**28** líquido para lavar vajilla
12 cazuela/cacerola	**29** paño para lavar platos
13 caldero	**30** tamiz o colador
14 bandeja	**31** paleta
15 caja del pan	**32** toalla para secar platos
16 estante	cloth
17 balanza	

1 aspirador	**10** cepillo para frotar
	11 plancha
2 escoba	**12** cable
3 tabla de planchar	**13** bombilla
4 máquina lavadora	**14** secador del pelo
5 fregasuelos	**15** enchufe
6 cepillo	**16** tomacorrientes
7 trapo	**17** interruptor
8 cogedor	**18** jabón en polvo
9 polvos para fregar	**19** cubo

	El Dormitorio		**20**	cepillo para el pelo
1	cama		**21**	peine
2	cabecera		**22**	pañuelos de papel
3	almohada		**23**	joyero
4	almohadón		**24**	reloj despertador
5	sábana		**25**	lámpara
6	manta			
7	colcha			El Bebé
8	colchón		**26**	cuna
9	mesilla		**27**	pijama
10	tocador		**28**	chupete
11	taburete		**29**	osito
12	espejo		**30**	sonajero
13	armarito		**31**	muñeca
14	armario		**32**	orinal de niño
15	cómoda		**33**	biberón
16	alfombra		**34**	tetilla
17	ropa		**35**	babero
18	cepillo de ropa		**36**	pañal
19	percha			

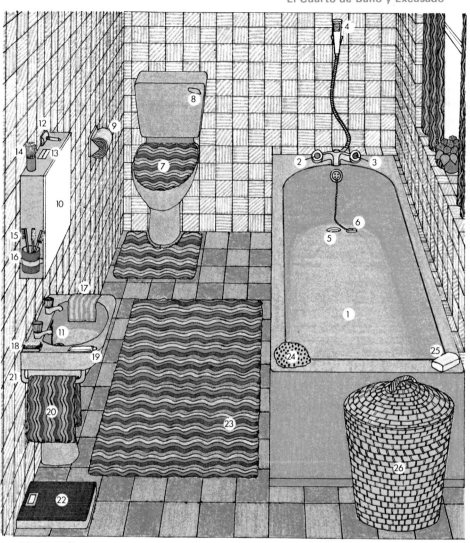

1	baño	**14**	brocha
2	grifo de agua caliente	**15**	cepillo de dientes
3	grifo de agua fría	**16**	vaso para los dientes
4	ducha	**17**	guante para la cara
5	desagüe	**18**	cepillo para las uñas
6	tapón	**19**	pasta dentífrica
7	retrete	**20**	toalla
8	empuñadura	**21**	toallero
9	papel higiénico	**22**	báscula
		23	estera de baño
10	armarito de cuarto de ba	**24**	esponja
11	lavabo	**25**	jabón
12	máquina de afeitar	**26**	cesto para la ropa
13	hoja de afeitar		

1	llanura/planicie	**11**	prado
2	montaña	**12**	río
3	cumbre/cima	**13**	campo
4	cascada	**14**	seto
5	lago	**15**	árbol
6	valle	**16**	pueblo
7	arroyo	**17**	senda
8	bosque	**18**	carretera
9	bosque extenso/selva	**19**	estanque
10	colina		

	Camping		**19**	hamaca
1	tienda		**20**	traje de baño
2	tela para el suelo			
3	saco para dormir		**21**	paletas para nadar
4	mochila		**22**	arena
5	estufa de camping		**23**	castillo de arena
			24	cubo
	En la Playa		**25**	pala
6	acantilado		**26**	pelota de playa
7	hotel		**27**	concha
8	chalet		**28**	piedras
9	paseo marítimo		**29**	rocas
10	rompeolas		**30**	cometa
11	playa		**31**	mar
12	sombrilla		**32**	espuma de ola
13	persona tomando el sol		**33**	ola
14	toalla de playa		**34**	motora
15	anteojos		**35**	nadador
16	snorkel		**36**	traje de baño
17	helado			
18	rompevientos		**37**	alga

1	henil	**19**	plough	arado
2	heno	**20**	furrow	surco
3	establo	**21**	cow	vaca
4	pajar	**22**	calf	ternera
5	corral	**23**	bull	toro
6	patio de la granja	**24**	goats	cabras
7	granja	**25**	beehive	colmena
8	campo	**26**	shepherd	pastor
9	estanque	**27**	crook	cayado de pastor
10	valla	**28**	sheepdog	perro pastor
11	árbol frutal	**29**	sheep	oveja
12	vergel	**30**	lamb	cordero
13	espantapájaros	**31**	duckling	patito
14	trigo	**32**	duck	pato
15	granjero	**33**	hen/chicken	gallina/pollo
16	cosechadora combinada	**34**	cock	gallo
17	canal de riego	**35**	chick	pollito
18	tractor			

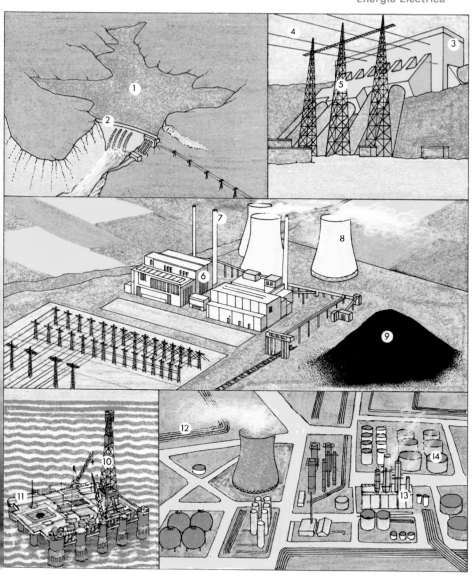

1	embalse	**8**	torre de enfriamiento
2	presa	**9**	combustible
3	casa de dínamos	**10**	torre petrolera
4	cable	**11**	instalación petrolera
5	torre metálica	**12**	oleoducto
6	central eléctrica	**13**	refineria
7	chimenea	**14**	depósito

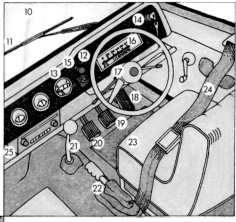

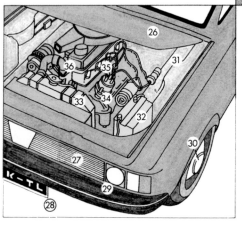

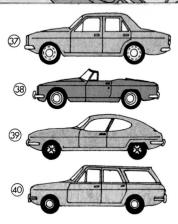

El automóvil

1	retrovisor	21	palanca de cambios
2	cofre	22	freno de mano
3	tapón de la gasolina	23	asiento
4	luz trasera	24	cinturón de seguridad
5	indicador luminoso	25	auto-radio
6	parachoques	26	capó
7	tubo de escape	27	rejilla del radiador
8	neumático	28	matrícula
9	antena	29	faro
10	parabrisas	30	tapacubos de rueda
11	limpiaparabrisas	31	motor
12	tablero de mandos	32	batería
13	indicador de combustible	33	radiador
14	encendido	34	distribuidor
15	estrangulador del aire	35	bujía
16	velocímetro	36	culata de cilindros
17	volante	37	automóvil de turismo
18	acelerador	38	descapotable
19	freno de pie	39	coupé o berlina
20	embrague	40	microbús/furgoneta

1 autopista	12 transportador
2 carretera elevada/paso	13 remolque de vivienda
3 cruce·subterráneo	14 camión
4 glorieta/redondel	15 ambulancia
5 carril exterior	16 coche
6 carril interior	17 autocar
7 gasolinera/estación de	18 automóvil deportivo
servicio	19 camión cisterna
8 surtidor de gasolina	20 motocicleta
9 bomba de aire	21 remolque
10 operario	22 camioneta
11 camión con remolque	

1	bicicleta	**20**	reflector
2	timbre	**21**	caballo
3	retrovisor	**22**	anteojeras
4	cable	**23**	arreos/guarniciones
5	faro	**24**	riendas
6	manillar	**25**	látigo
7	sillín	**26**	carreta
8	bolsa de sillín	**27**	casco
9	rueda	**28**	gafas
10	guardabarros	**29**	scúter
11	neumático	**30**	luz trasera
12	radios	**31**	asiento
13	válvula	**32**	acelerador
14	freno	**33**	freno
15	barra transversal	**34**	cesto
16	bomba	**35**	tubo de escape
17	pedal	**36**	arranque
18	cadena	**37**	soporte
19	pasador	**38**	palanca de cambios

1	tren	17	barrera
2	conductor	18	sala de espera
3	locomotora	19	pasajeros
4	coche	20	andén
5	compartimiento	21	número de andén
6	inspector de billetes	22	operario de señales
7	billete	23	caseta de señales
8	asiento	24	linea de ferrocarril
9	rejilla portamaletas	25	traviesas
10	jefe de tren	26	agujas
11	bandera	27	señales
12	pito	28	vagón de mercancias
13	estación	29	parachoques
14	taquilla/despacho	30	aparcadero
15	horario		
16	inspector		

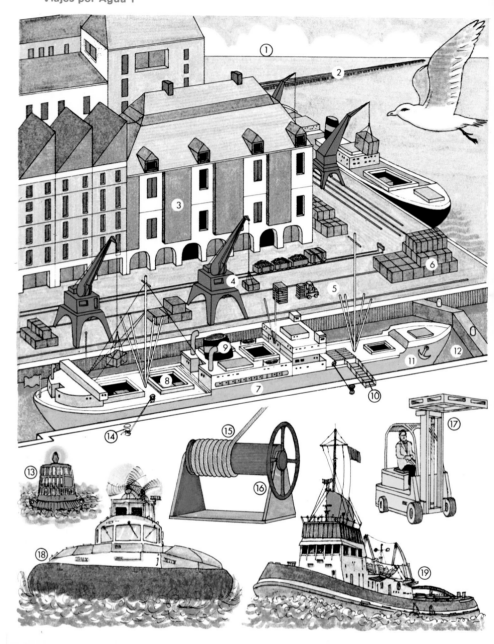

1 horizonte	11 ancla
2 malecón	12 atracadero
3 almacén	13 boya
4 grúa	14 pita de amarrar
5 muelle	15 cable
6 carga	16 molinete
7 barco	17 carretón de horquilla elevador
8 bodega/cala	18 aerodeslizador
9 chimenea	19 remolcador
0 pasarela	

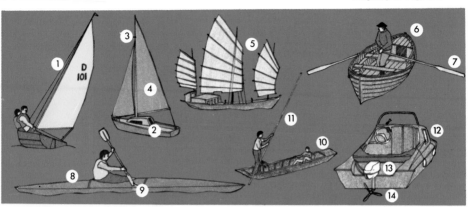

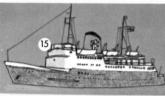

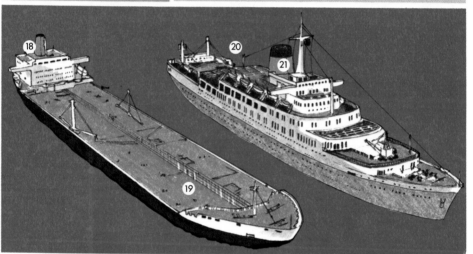

1	yate	**12**	lancha motora
2	embarcación con cabi	**13**	motor fuera de borda
3	mástil	**14**	hélice
4	vela	**15**	transbordador
5	junco	**16**	barcaza
6	embarcación de remos	**17**	trainera
7	remo	**18**	buque cisterna
8	canoa	**19**	cubierta
9	paleta	**20**	transatlántico
10	barca de fondo plano	**21**	chimenea
11	poste		

1	sala de aduanas	**12**	motor a reacción
2	aduanero	**13**	timón de cola
3	pasaporte	**14**	planeador
4	equipaje	**15**	helicóptero
5	capitán	**16**	rotor
6	pasajero	**17**	avión ligero
7	azafata	**18**	hélice
8	camarero aéreo	**19**	pista de aterrizaje
9	aeroplano/avión	**20**	torre de control
10	fuselaje	**21**	hangar
11	ala		

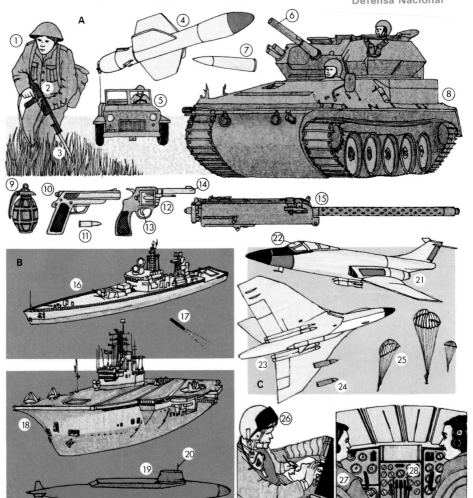

A. Ejército
1 soldado
2 fusil
3 bayoneta
4 misil teledirigido
5 jeep
6 cañón
7 obús
8 tanque
9 granada de mano
10 pistola
11 bala
12 revólver
13 gatillo
14 cañón
15 ametralladora

B. Marina
16 buque de guerra
17 torpedo
18 portaviones
19 submarino
20 periscopio

C. Fuerzas Aéreas
21 avión de combate
22 carlinga
23 bombardero
24 bomba
25 paracaídas
26 navegador
27 piloto
28 panel de control

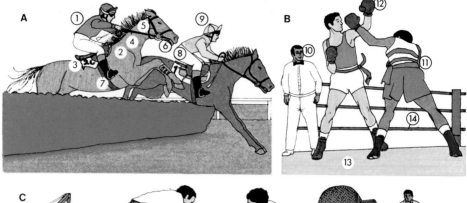

(Horse-)racing	A.	Carreras de Caballos
jockey	1	jinete
(race-)horse	2	caballo de carreras
saddle	3	silla
reins	4	riendas
bridle	5	brida
bit	6	bocado
stirrup	7	estribo
riding breeches/	8	pantalones de montar a
jodhpurs		caballo
cap	9	gorro

Boxing	B.	Boxeo
referee	10	árbitro
boxer	11	boxeador
glove	12	guante
ring	13	ring
ropes	14	cuerdas

Basketball	C.	Baloncesto
basket	15	cesta

backboard	16	tablero de soporte
ball	17	pelota

Hockey	D.	Hockey
stick	18	bastón

Table-tennis	E.	Ping-Pong
bat	19	pala
net	20	red
table	21	mesa

Wrestling	F.	Lucha libre
wrestlers	22	luchadores

Judo	G.	Yudo
judo suit	23	traje de yudo

Rugby	H.	Rugby
player	24	jugador
goal	25	gol

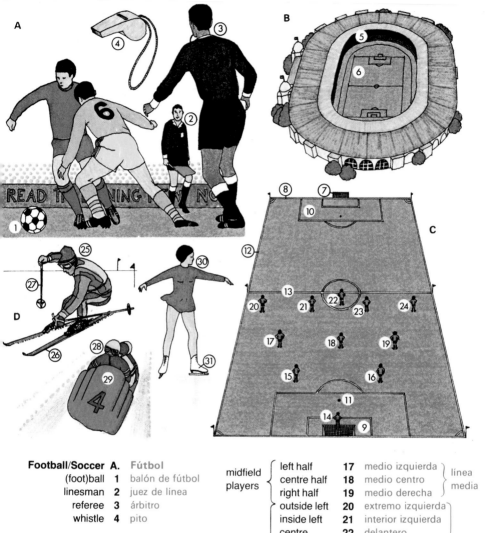

Football/Soccer	A.	Fútbol					
(foot)ball	1	balón de fútbol	midfield	left half	17	medio izquierda	línea
linesman	2	juez de línea	players	centre half	18	medio centro	media
referee	3	árbitro		right half	19	medio derecha	
whistle	4	pito		outside left	20	extremo izquierda	
				inside left	21	interior izquierda	
				centre	22	delantero	
Stadium	B.	Estadio	strikers	forward		centro	delante
stand	5	tribuna		inside right	23	interior derecha	
pitch/field	6	campo		outside right	24	extremo derecha	

Line-up	C.	Alineación		Winter Sports	D.	Deportes de invierno
goal	7	gol		skier	25	esquiador
goal-line	8	línea de gol		ski	26	esquí
goal area	9	zona de gol		(ski-)stick/pole	27	bastón de esquí
penalty area	10	zona de penalty		tobogganist	28	corredor en trineo
penalty spot	11	punto de penalty		toboggan	29	trineo
touch line	12	línea de banda		skater	30	patinador
halfway line	13	línea media		skate	31	patín
goalkeeper	14	guardameta portero				

defenders { left back 15 defensa izquierda } línea de
{ right back 16 defensa derecha } defensa

Baseball **A.**	Baseball	umpire **16**	
catcher **1**	receptor	crease **17**	
mask **2**	máscara		
glove **3**	guante	**Fishing C.**	Pesca
bat **4**	pala	fisherman **18**	pescador
batter **5**	golpeador	rod **19**	caña
		line **20**	hilo
Cricket B.	Cricket	hook **21**	anzuelo
batsman **6**	Las expresiones	bait **22**	cebo
bat **7**	relativas al juego de		
bails **8**	cricket no tienen		
wicket/stumps **9**	equivalente en	**Tennis D.**	Tenis
cricket ball **10**	castellano	(tennis-)court **23**	pista de tenis
wicket-keeper **11**		net **24**	red
pad **12**		server **25**	jugador que saca
pitch **13**		service line **26**	línea de saque
bowler **14**		racket **27**	raqueta
fielder **15**		tennis-ball **28**	pelota de tenis/bola

Orchestra	Orquesta		pedal **17**	pedal
flute **1**	flauta		stool **18**	taburete
clarinet **2**	clarinete		trumpet **19**	trompeta
musician/player **3**	músico		trombone **20**	trombón
violin **4**	violín		slide **21**	vara
strings **5**	cuerdas		saxophone **22**	saxofón
bow **6**	arco		mouthpiece **23**	boquilla
viola **7**	viola			
cello **8**	violoncelo		**Pop Group**	**Grupo Pop**
double-bass **9**	contrabajo		singer **24**	cantante
conductor **10**	director		microphone/mike **25**	micrófono
baton **11**	batuta		(electric) guitar **26**	guitarra eléctrica
(sheet) music **12**	partitura		amplifier **27**	amplificador
rostrum **13**	plataforma del director		loudspeaker **28**	altavoz
horn **14**	trompa		cymbals **29**	címbalos
piano **15**	piano		drum **30**	tambor
keys **16**	teclas			

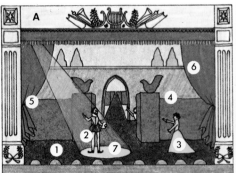
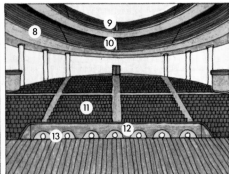

A. El Teatro
1 escena
2 actor
3 actriz
4 decorados
5 bastidores
6 cortinas
7 foco
8 teatro
9 galería
10 anfiteatro
11 butacas
12 foso de orquesta
13 candilejas

B. El Cine
14 sala de proyección
15 proyector
16 operario de proyección
17 cine/sala
18 pantalla
19 acomodadora
20 asientos
21 pasillo

C. La Biblioteca
22 bibliotecario
23 índice de tarjetas
24 mostrador
25 estantería

1	botella	**17**	moza de bar
2	tapón de botella	**18**	barman
3	jarra	**19**	bomba
4	lata	**20**	taburete
5	caja de cerillas	**21**	camarero
6	cerilla	**22**	cliente
7	abrebotellas	**23**	menú
8	cigarrillo	**24**	botella de vino
9	ceniza	**25**	corcho
10	cenicero	**26**	vaso de vino
11	sacacorchos	**27**	salero
12	paja	**28**	mostacero
13	bebida no alcohólica	**29**	pimentero
14	jarro	**30**	mantel
15	tocadiscos automático	**31**	servilleta
16	bar		

Chess and Draughts	A.	Ajedrez y Damas
(set of) chessmen/	1	juego de piezas de
chess pieces		ajedrez
board	2	tablero
pawn	3	peón
rook/castle	4	castillo
knight	5	caballo
bishop	6	alfil
queen	7	reina
king	8	rey
draughts	9	damas

Cards	B.	Naipes
(pack of)	10	baraja de naipes
(playing-)cards		
jack/knave of clubs	11	sota de bastos
queen of diamonds	12	reina de diamantes
king of hearts	13	rey de corazones
ace of spades	14	as de espadas

Reading	C.	Lectura
book	15	libro
cover	16	cubierta
(dust-)jacket	17	guardapolvos
spine	18	lomo
page	19	página
illustration	20	ilustración
text	21	texto

Photography	D.	Fotografía
print/photograph/	22	fotografía/foto
photo/snapshot		
negative	23	negativo
(roll of) film	24	rollo de película
camera	25	cámara fotográfica
lens	26	lente
screen	27	pantalla
stand	28	trípode
(slide-)projector	29	proyector
slide	30	diapositiva

sewing-machine	**1**	máquina de coser	button	**15**	botón
tape	**2**	cinta	button-hole	**16**	ojal
seam	**3**	costura	stitch	**17**	puntada
hem	**4**	dobladillo	knitting-needle	**18**	aguja de hacer punto
thimble	**5**	dedal	wool	**19**	lana
needle	**6**	aguja	pattern	**20**	patrón
elastic	**7**	cinta elástica	knitting	**21**	punto
reel of cotton	**8**	carrete de hilo	zip/zipper/zip-	**22**	cremallera
lace	**9**	encaje	fastener		
safety-pin	**10**	imperdible	hook and eye	**23**	gancho y ojete
pleat	**11**	pliegue	ribbon	**24**	cinta
pin	**12**	alfiler	tape-measure	**25**	cinta de medida/metro
material/cloth	**13**	tejido/tela	scissors	**26**	tijeras
frill	**14**	volante	press-stud	**27**	botón de presión

1 peluquero	9 mecanógrafa
2 carnicero	10 costurera
3 carpintero	11 camarera
4 empleado de banco	12 conductor
5 mecánico	13 payaso
6 cargador de muelle	14 mozo de carga
7 minero	15 anunciador/locutor
8 artista	

1 verdulero	**9** vendedor
2 electricista	**10** enfermera
3 jardinero	**11** maestro
4 fotógrafo	**12** soldado
5 florista	**13** policía
6 barbero	**14** óptico
7 panadero	**15** marinero
8 doctor/médico	

horse	**1**	caballo	puppy **14**	cachorro/perrezno
foal	**2**	potrillo	cat **15**	gato
pig	**3**	cerdo/puerco	kitten **16**	gatito
snout	**4**	hocico	paw **17**	pata
llama	**5**	llama	mouse **18**	ratón
camel	**6**	camello	squirrel **19**	ardilla
hump	**7**	joroba	rabbit **20**	conejo
buffalo	**8**	búfalo	whisker **21**	bigote/barba
horn	**9**	cuerno	rat **22**	rata
donkey	**10**	burro/asno	tail **23**	cola
reindeer	**11**	reno	fox **24**	zorra
antler	**12**	asta	bat **25**	murciélago
dog	**13**	perro	hedgehog **26**	puerco espín/erizo

whale	**1**	ballena	
fluke	**2**	aleta de ballena	
dolphin	**3**	delfín	
fin	**4**	aleta	
antelope	**5**	antílope	
kangaroo	**6**	canguro	
pouch	**7**	bolsa	
bear	**8**	oso	
seal	**9**	foca	
flipper	**10**	aleta	
wolf	**11**	lobo	
baboon	**12**	babuíno	
monkey	**13**	mono	
gorilla	**14**	gorila	
giraffe	**15**	jirafa	
lion	**16**	león	
mane	**17**	melena	
leopard	**18**	leopardo	
tiger	**19**	tigre	
hippopotamus	**20**	hipopótamo	
elephant	**21**	elefante	
trunk	**22**	trompa	
tusk	**23**	colmillo	
zebra	**24**	cebra	
rhinoceros	**25**	rinoceronte	
horn	**26**	cuerno	

Fish and other		**Peces y otros**	shell	**14**	concha
animals		**animales**	sunfish	**15**	rueda
shark	**1**	tiburón	oyster	**16**	ostra
fin	**2**	aleta	crab	**17**	cangrejo
swordfish	**3**	pez espada	pincer/claw	**18**	pinza/tenaza
salmon	**4**	salmón	slug	**19**	babosa
gill	**5**	agalla/branquia	frog	**20**	rana
herring	**6**	arenque	worm	**21**	gusano
tail	**7**	cola	centipede	**22**	ciempiés
mouth	**8**	boca	octopus	**23**	pulpo
scales	**9**	escamas	tentacle	**24**	tentáculo
eel	**10**	anguila	spider	**25**	araña
jelly-fish	**11**	medusa	(cob)web	**26**	tela de araña/telaraña
lobster	**12**	langosta	scorpion	**27**	escorpión
snail	**13**	caracol			

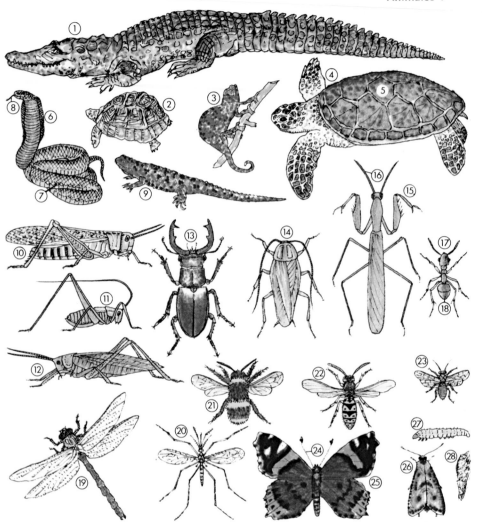

Reptiles A.		Reptiles
crocodile	1	cocodrilo
tortoise	2	tortuga
chameleon	3	camaleón
turtle	4	tortuga de mar
shell	5	caparazón
snake	6	serpiente
coil	7	espiral
tongue	8	lengua
lizard	9	lagarto
Insects B.		**Insectos**
locust	10	langosta
cricket	11	grillo
grasshopper	12	saltamonte
beetle	13	escarabajo

cockroach	14	cucaracha
mantis	15	mantis religiosa
feeler	16	antena
ant	17	hormiga
abdomen	18	abdomen
dragonfly	19	libélula
mosquito	20	mosquito
bee	21	abeja
wasp	22	avispa
fly	23	mosca
antenna	24	antena
butterfly	25	mariposa
moth	26	polilla
caterpillar	27	oruga
cocoon	28	capullo

Birds		Aves			
ostrich	1	avestruz	canary	18	canario
eagle	2	águila	bill	19	pico
claw	3	garra	parrot	20	loro
beak	4	pico	(sea)gull	21	gaviota
feathers	5	plumas	swallow	22	golondrina
hawk	6	halcón	wing	23	ala
owl	7	buho	dove	24	paloma
flamingo	8	flamenco	goose	25	ganso
webbed foot	9	palmípedo	budgerigar	26	periquito
vulture	10	buitre	humming-bird	27	colibrí
peacock	11	pavo real	sparrow	28	gorrión
crest	12	cresta	nest	29	nido
penguin	13	pingüino	kingfisher	30	martin pescador
pheasant	14	faisán	pigeon	31	pichón
heron	15	garza real	blackbird	32	mirlo
turkey	16	pavo	crow	33	cuervo
swan	17	cisne			

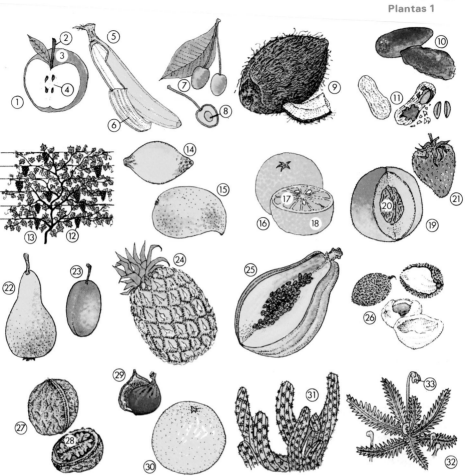

Fruit		Fruta
apple	**1**	manzana
stalk	**2**	rabo
peel	**3**	piel
core	**4**	corazón
banana	**5**	plátano
skin	**6**	piel
cherry	**7**	cereza
stone	**8**	hueso
coconut	**9**	coco
date	**10**	dátil
peanut/groundnut	**11**	cacahuete
grapes	**12**	uvas
vine	**13**	viña
lemon	**14**	limón
mango	**15**	mango
orange	**16**	naranja
segments	**17**	gajos

peel/rind	**18**	piel/mondadura
peach	**19**	melocotón
stone	**20**	hueso
strawberry	**21**	fresa
pear	**22**	pera
plum	**23**	ciruela
pineapple	**24**	piña/ananás
pawpaw/papaya	**25**	papaya
lychee	**26**	lychee
walnut	**27**	nuez
kernel	**28**	semilla
fig	**29**	higo
grapefruit	**30**	pomelo
cactus	**31**	cactus
fern	**32**	helecho
frond	**33**	fronda

Vegetables		Vegetales
bean	**1**	habichuela
stalk	**2**	rabo
pea	**3**	guisante
pod	**4**	vaina
carrot	**5**	zanahoria
potato	**6**	patata
marrow	**7**	calabacín
cucumber	**8**	pepino
beetroot	**9**	remolacha
cauliflower	**10**	coliflor
cabbage	**11**	col/repollo/berza
lettuce	**12**	lechuga
onion	**13**	cebolla
mushroom	**14**	seta
tomato	**15**	tomate
aubergine/eggplant	**16**	berenjena

Flowers		Flores
daffodil	**17**	narciso trompón
daisy	**18**	margarita
rose	**19**	rosa
petal	**20**	pétalo
orchid	**21**	orquídea
tulip	**22**	tulipán
stem	**23**	tallo
hibiscus	**24**	hibisco
bud	**25**	capullo
waterlily	**26**	nenúfar
sunflower	**27**	girasol
seeds	**28**	semillas

corn/maize	**1**	maíz	
ear of wheat	**2**	espiga de trigo	
olive	**3**	aceituna	
cocoa pod	**4**	cápsula de cacao	
coffee berry	**5**	grano de café	
cotton	**6**	algodón	
rice	**7**	arroz	
tea	**8**	té	
sugar-cane	**9**	caña de azúcar	
oak tree	**10**	roble	
roots	**11**	raíces	
trunk	**12**	tronco	
branch/bough	**13**	rama	
twig	**14**	ramita	
leaf	**15**	hoja	
acorn	**16**	bellota	
bark	**17**	corteza	
log	**18**	tronco de madero	
palm	**19**	palmera	
fir	**20**	abeto	
cone	**21**	piña	
needles	**22**	agujas	
cedar	**23**	cedro	
willow	**24**	sauce	

blow **1** soplar	dream **14** soñar	
break **2** romper	drive **15** conducir	
carry **3** llevar	drown **16** ahogarse	
catch **4** agarrar	eat **17** comer	
climb **5** subir/trepar	fall **18** caer	
crawl **6** arrastrarse/serpentear	fight **19** luchar	
cry/weep **7** llorar/sollozar	fly **20** volar	
cut **8** cortar	jump/leap **21** soltar/brincar	
dance **9** bailar	kick **22** dar puntapiés	
dig **10** cavar/excavar	kneel **23** arrodillarse	
dive **11** bucear	laugh **24** reir	
draw **12** dibujar	lick **25** lamer	
drink **13** beber		

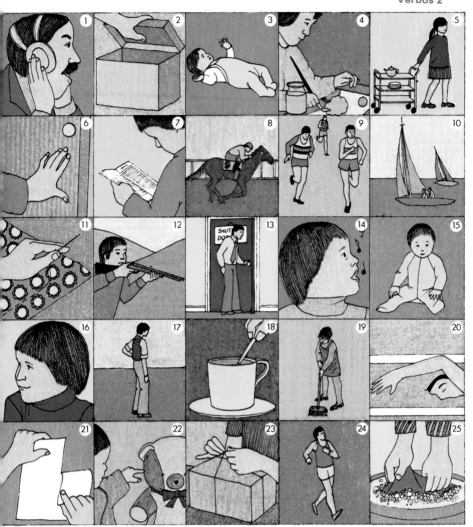

listen **1** escuchar	sing **14** cantar
open **2** abrir	sit **15** sentarse
lie **3** yacer	smile **16** sonreir
paint **4** pintar	stand **17** ponerse de pie
pull **5** tirar	stir **18** remover
push **6** empujar	sweep **19** barrer
read **7** leer	swim **20** nadar
ride **8** cabalgar	tear **21** romper/rasgar
run **9** correr	touch **22** tocar
sail **10** navegar	tie **23** atar
sew **11** coser	walk **24** caminar/pasear
shoot **12** disparar	wash **25** lavar
shut **13** cerrar	

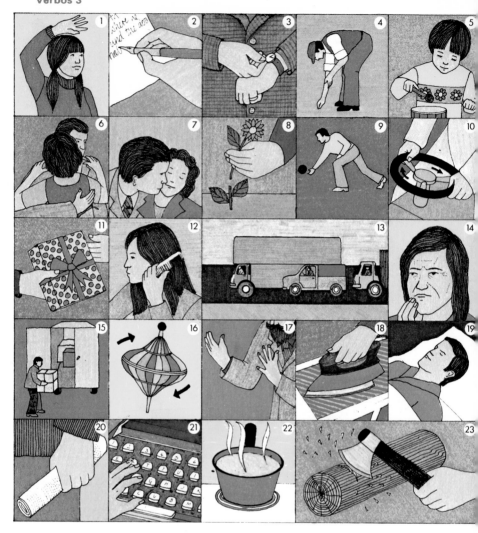

wave **1** agitar la mano	pass/overtake **13** pasar
write **2** escribir	frown **14** fruncir
wind **3** dar cuerda al reloj	put **15** poner
bend **4** doblar	spin **16** girar
hit/beat **5** golpear	clap **17** aplaudir
hug **6** abrazar	iron **18** planchar
kiss **7** besar	sleep **19** dormir
pick **8** coger	hold **20** tener en la mano
throw **9** arrojar	type **21** escribir a máquina
turn **10** girar/dar vueltas	boil **22** hervir
give **11** dar	chop **23** cortar
comb **12** peinar	

carton	**1**	caja de cartón	crate	**11**	caja
urn	**2**	urna	trunk	**12**	baúl
briefcase	**3**	cartera	sack	**13**	saco
barrel	**4**	barril	cage	**14**	jaula
(hand)bag	**5**	bolso	carrier-bag	**15**	bolsa de papel
purse	**6**	monedero	wallet	**16**	cartera
paper-bag	**7**	bolsa de papel	(suit)case	**17**	maleta
dustbin	**8**	cubo de basura	holdall	**18**	neceser
thermos/vacuum-flask	**9**	termos	box	**19**	caja
(shopping) basket	**10**	cesta para la compra	safe	**20**	caja fuerte
			(water-)tank	**21**	depósito de agua

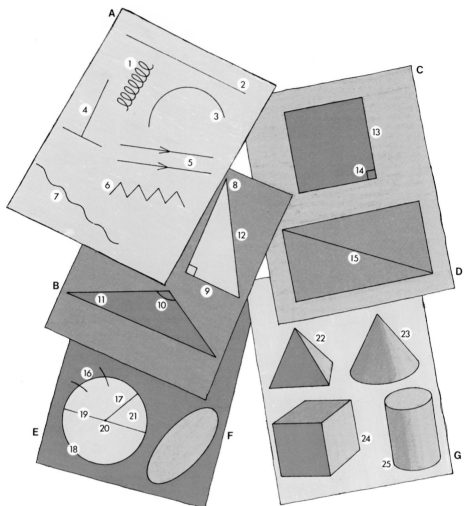

Lines **A.**	Líneas	Rectangle/Oblong **D.**	Rectángulo
spiral **1**	espiral	diagonal **15**	diagonal
straight line **2**	línea recta		
curve **3**	curva	Circle **E.**	Círculo
perpendicular line **4**	línea perpendicular	arc **16**	arco
parallel lines **5**	líneas paralelas	radius **17**	radio
zig-zag **6**	zigzag	circumference **18**	circunferencia
wavy line **7**	línea ondulada	diameter **19**	diámetro
		centre **20**	centro
Triangles **B.**	Triángulos	section **21**	sector
apex **8**	vértice		
base **9**	base	Oval/Ellipse **F.**	Ovalo/elipse
obtuse angle **10**	ángulo obtuso		
acute angle **11**	ángulo agudo	Solid Figures **G.**	Sólidos
hypotenuse **12**	hipotenusa	pyramid **22**	pirámide
		cone **23**	cono
Square **C.**	Cuadrado	cube **24**	cubo
side **13**	lado	cylinder **25**	cilindro
right angle **14**	ángulo recto		

top	**1**	arriba	a half	**12**	una mitad
bottom	**2**	abajo	a third	**13**	un tercio
corner	**3**	esquina	a quarter	**14**	un cuarto
edge	**4**	borde	plus	**15**	más
side	**5**	lado	multiplied by	**16**	multiplicado por
back	**6**	fondo	minus	**17**	menos
front	**7**	frente	divided by	**18**	dividido por
width	**8**	anchura	equals	**19**	iguala a
height	**9**	altura	per cent	**20**	por ciento
depth	**10**	profundidad	decimal point	**21**	coma decimal
length	**11**	longitud	fraction	**22**	fracción

The Time A. La Hora

minute hand	1	minutero	
hour hand	2	manilla de las horas	
second hand	3	segundero	
clock face	4	esfera del reloj	
9:00: nine o'clock	5	9.00: las nueve	
9:10: ten past nine/nine ten	6	9.10: las nueve y diez	
9:15: (a) quarter past nine/nine fifteen	7	9.15: las nueve y cuarto/las nueve y quince	
9:30: half past nine/nine thirty	8	9.30: las nueve y media/las nueve y treinta	
9:45: a quarter to ten/nine forty-five	9	9.45: las diez menos cuarto/las nueve cuarenta y ci	
9:50: ten to ten/nine fifty	10	9.50: las diez menos diez/las nueve cincuenta	

The Date B. La Fecha

calendar **11** calendario

Today's date is Wednesday the sixteenth of July, nineteen eighty: 16th July 1980 or 16/7/80.

La fecha de hoy es miércoles, dieciséis de julio de mil novecientos ochenta: 16 de julio de 1980 o 16/7/80.

The Temperature C. La Temperatura

thermometer **12** termómetro

The temperature is 18 degrees centigrade (18°C) or 65 degrees Fahrenheit (65°F).

La temperatura es de 18 grados centígrados (18 C) o 65 grados farenheit (65 F)

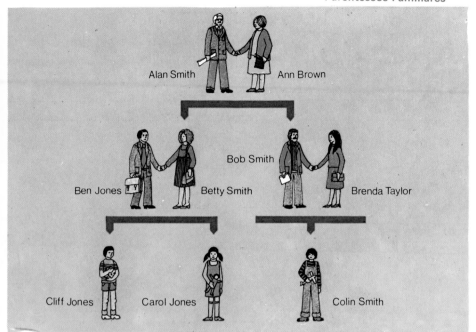

1 Alan and Ann are **husband** and **wife**.
2 Their **children** are Betty and Bob.
3 Their **daughter** is Betty and their **son** is Bob.
4 Alan is Bob's **father** and Ann is Bob's **mother**.
5 Betty is Bob's **sister** and Bob is Betty's **brother**.
6 Alan is Ben's **father-in-law** and Ann is his **mother-in-law**.
7 Ben is Alan and Ann's **son-in-law** and Brenda is their **daughter-in-law**.
8 Ben is Bob's **brother-in-law** and Brenda is Betty's **sister-in-law**.
9 Colin is Cliff and Carol's **cousin**.
10 Betty is Colin's **aunt** and Ben is his **uncle**.
11 Colin is Betty's **nephew** and Carol is Bob's **niece**.
12 Cliff is Ann and Alan's **grandson** and Carol is their **granddaughter**.

1 Alan y Ann son **marido** y **esposa**
2 .Sus **hijos** son Betty y Bob
3 Su **hija** es Betty y su **hijo** es Bob
4 Alan es el **padre** de Bob y Ann es la **madre** de Bob
5 Betty es la **hermana** de Bob y Bob es el **hermano** de Betty
6 Alan es el **suegro** de Ben y Ann es su **suegra**
7 Ben es el **yerno** de Alan y Ann y Brenda es su **nuera**
8 Ben es el **cuñado** de Bob y Brenda es la **cuñada** de Betty
9 Colin es el **primo** de Cliff y Carol
10 Betty es la **tía** de Colin y Ben es su **tío**
11 Colin es el **sobrino** de Betty y Carol es la **sobrina** de Bob
12 Cliff es el **nieto** de Ann y Alan y Carol es su **nieta**

bunch (of flowers) **1**	ramo (de flores)	heap (of stones) **9**	montón (de piedras)

bunch (of flowers) **1** ramo (de flores)
bundle (of sticks) **2** manojo (de leña)
crowd (of people) **3** muchedumbre
fleet (of ships) **4** flota (de naves)
flight (of stairs) **5** tramo (de escaleras)
flock (of sheep or **6** rebaño (de ovejas)/
  birds) bandada (de pájaros)
gang (of workmen) **7** cuadrilla
string (of beads) **8** sarta (de abalorios)

heap (of stones) **9** montón (de piedras)
herd (of cows) **10** rebaño (de ganado)
party (of tourists) **11** grupo (de turistas)
pile (of blankets) **12** montón (de frazados)
plate (of sandwiches) **13** plato (de bocadillos)
row (of houses) **14** fila (de casas)
team (of players) **15** equipo (de jugadores)
swarm (of bees) **16** enjambre (de abejas)

ball (of string, wool)	1	ovillo (de hilo, lana)	
bar (of chocolate)	2	barra (de chocolate)	
tablet/bar (of soap)	3	tableta/barra (de jabón)	
joint (of meat)	4	cuarto (de carne)	
line (of washing)	5	cuerda (de ropa)	
loaf (of bread)	6	pan	
lump (of sugar)	7	terrón/trozo (de azúcar)	
slice/piece (of cake)	8	rebanada/trozo (de torta)	

reel (of cotton)	9	carrete (de hilo)	
box (of matches)/	10	caja (de cerillas)/	
packet (of cigarettes)		cajetilla (de cigarrillos)	
packet (of tea)	11	paquete (de té)	
roll (of paper)	12	rollo (de papel)	
tube (of toothpaste)	13	(tubo de) dentrífico	
bowl (of soup)	14	fuente (de sopa)	

1	a) grande/amplio	**9**	a) rápido
	b) pequeño/menudo		b) lento
2	a) mellado	**10**	a) ~~grueso~~ gordo
	b) afilado		b) delgado
3	a) limpio	**11**	a) feliz
	b) sucio		b) triste
4	a) cerrado	**12**	a) fácil
	b) abierto		b) difícil/duro
5	a) torcido	**13**	a) blando
	b) derecho		b) duro
6	a) poco hondo	**14**	a) alto
	b) profundo		b) bajo
7	a) mojado	**15**	a) caliente
	b) seco		b) frío
8	a) vacío	**16**	a) largo
	b) lleno		b) corto

1	a) estrecho	9	a) bonito/hermoso
	b) ancho		b) feo
2	a) joven	10	a) primero
	b) viejo		b) último
3	a) nuevo	11	a) claro
	b) viejo		b) oscuro
4	a) tranquilo	12	a) ligero
	b) agitado		b) pesado
5	a) áspero	13	a) ruidoso
	b) suave		b) suave
6	a) fuerte	14	a) macizo
	b) débil		b) hueco
7	a) ordenado	15	a) grueso
	b) desordenado		b) delgado
8	a) bueno	16	a) suelto
	b) malo		b) apretado

1	**fuera** de la habitación	11	**fuera del** cajón
2	**a través** de la puerta	12	**en** la mesa
3	**debajo** del cuadro	13	**en/sobre** la mesa
4	**abajo** de la pared	14	**junto/próximo a** la
5	**arriba** de la pared		mesa
6	**alrededor** del cuello	15	**junto a/cerca de** la si
7	**delante** de la silla	16	**detrás** de la silla
8	**contra** la pared	17	**bajo/debajo de** la
9	**en** el cajón		mesa
10	**en/dentro** del cajón		

1 **por encima** de los árboles	**8** **en** la esquina
2 **más allá** del puente	**9** **a lo largo de** la carretera
3 **del** mar	**10** **hacia** el puente
4 **al** mar	**11** **alejado del** puente
5 **entre** los árboles	
6 **fuera de** la carretera	**12** **entre** los coches
7 **a través/sobre** la carretera	

A. **This** boy is Paul. **He** is holding **his** football. **It** is **his**. He says, "I am Paul. **This** is **my** football. It is **mine**. **Its** colours are black and white."

B. This girl is Mary. **She** is riding **her** bicycle. It is **hers**. She says, "My father gave it to **me**."

C. Paul and Mary have a dog. He is **theirs**. **They** are feeding **their** dog. Bob is watching **them**. Mary says to Bob, "This is **our** dog. He is **ours**. He belongs to **us**. **We** are feeding **him**." Bob says, "This is water for **your** dog."

D. Paul says to Bob, "**Who** is **that** girl **there?**" Bob says, "**That** is Julie. She is coming **here**."

E. Bob says to Julie. "**What** are **those** things **you** are carrying?" Julie says, "**These** are oranges." Paul says, "**Whose** oranges are they?" Julie says, "They are for **you** and Bob. They are **yours**." Bob says, "**Which one** is mine?" Julie says, "This one here. But **where** is Mary? **This** one is for **her**."

A. **Este** muchacho es Pablo. **Él** tiene **su** balón. Es **el suyo**. **Él** dice, "**Yo** soy Pablo. **Éste** es **mi** balón. Es **el mío**. **Sus** colores son blanco y negro."

B. **Esta** muchacha es María. **Ella** va en **su** bicicleta. Es la **suya**. Ella dice, "Mi padre me la dio a **mí**."

C. Pablo y María tienen un perro. El perro es **suyo**. **Ellos** dan de comer a **su** perro. Bob **les** está mirando. María le dice a Bob, "Este es **nuestro** perro. Es **el nuestro**. **Nos** pertenece. **Le** estamos dando de comer". Bob dice, "Aquí tenéis agua para **vuestro** perro."

D. Pablo le dice a Bob, "**¿Quién** es **esa** muchacha que está **allí?**" Bob dice, "**Ésa** es Julie. Viene **aquí**."

E. Bob le dice a Julie, "**¿Qué** son **esas** cosas que **tú** llevas?" Julie dice, "**Éstas** son naranjas". Pablo dice "**¿De quién** son las naranjas?". Julie dice, "Son para **ti** y Bob. Son **las vuestras**". Bob dice, "**¿Cuál** es la mía?" Julie dice, "Ésta de aquí. Pero **¿dónde** está María? **Ésta** es para **ella**."

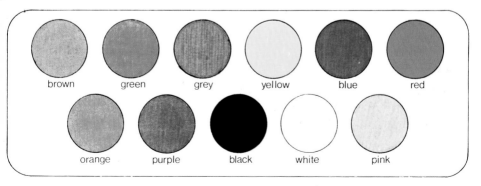

brown	green	grey	yellow	blue	red
marrón	verde	gris	amarillo	azul	rojo
orange	purple	black	white	pink	
naranja	púrpura	negro	blanco	rosa	

Numerals
Números cardinales

nought, zero, nothing	**0**	nada/cero
one	**1**	uno
two	**2**	dos
three	**3**	tres
four	**4**	cuatro
five	**5**	cinco
six	**6**	seis
seven	**7**	siete
eight	**8**	ocho
nine	**9**	nueve
ten	**10**	diez
eleven	**11**	once
twelve	**12**	doce
thirteen	**13**	trece
fourteen	**14**	catorce
fifteen	**15**	quince
sixteen	**16**	dieciséis
seventeen	**17**	diecisiete
eighteen	**18**	dieciocho
nineteen	**19**	diecinueve
twenty	**20**	veinte
twenty-one	**21**	veintiuno
thirty	**30**	treinta

forty	**40**		cuarenta
fifty	**50**		cincuenta
sixty	**60**		sesenta
seventy	**70**		setenta
eighty	**80**		ochenta
ninety	**90**		noventa
a/one hundred	**100**		cien
five hundred	**500**		quinientos
six hundred and	**621**		seiscientos
twenty-one			seiscientos veintiuno
a/one thousand	**1,000**		mil
a million	**1,000,000**		un millón
first	**1st**	1°	primero
second	**2nd**	2°	segundo
third	**3rd**	3°	tercero
fourth	**4th**	4°	cuarto
fifth	**5th**	5°	quinto
sixth	**6th**	6°	sexto
seventh	**7th**	7°	séptimo
eighth	**8th**	8°	octavo
ninth	**9th**	9°	noveno
tenth	**10th**	10°	décimo
twentieth	**20th**	20°	vigésimo

Weight
1,000 grams (g) = 1 kilogram (kg)

Peso
1.000 gramos (g) = 1 kilogramo (kg)

Length
10 millimetres (mm) = 1 centimetre (cm)
100 centimetres = 1 metre (m)
1,000 metres = 1 kilometre (km)

Longitud
10 milímetros (mm) = 1 centímetro (cm)
100 centímetros = 1 metro (m)
1.000 metros = 1 kilómetro (km)

Liquids
1,000 millilitres (ml) = 1 litre (l)

Líquidos
1.000 mililitros (ml) = 1 litro (l)

Time
60 seconds = 1 minute (min)
60 minutes = 1 hour (hr)
24 hours = 1 day
7 days = 1 week (wk)
365 days = 1 year (yr)
12 months = 1 year
100 years = 1 century (c)

Hora
60 segundos = 1 minuto (min)
60 minutos = 1 hora (h)
24 horas = 1 día
7 días = 1 semana
365 días = 1 año
12 meses = 1 año
100 años = 1 siglo

Days of the Week
Días de la Semana

Monday, Tuesday, Wednesday, Thursday, Friday, Saturday, Sunday

lunes, martes, miércoles, jueves, viernes, sábado y domingo.

Months of the Year
Meses del Año

January, February, March, April, May, June, July, August, September, October, November, December.

enero, febrero, marzo, abril, mayo, junio, julio, agosto, septiembre, octubre, noviembre, diciembre.

Vocales y Diptongos
Pronunciación y Acentuación

i: como en *sea* /siː/
ɪ como en *sit* /sɪt/
e como en *ten* /ten/
æ como en *hat* /hæt/
ɑː como en *farm* /fɑːm/
ɒ como en *pot* /pɒt/
ɔː como en *ball* /bɔːl/

ʊ como en *book* /bʊk/
uː como en *root* /ruːt/
ʌ como en *cup* /kʌp/
ɜː como en *fur* /fɜː(r)/
ə como en *away* /əˈweɪ/
eɪ como en *page* /peɪdʒ/
əʊ como en *hole* /həʊl/

aɪ como en *five* /faɪv/
aʊ como en *mouse* /maʊs/
ɔɪ como en *toy* /tɔɪ/
ɪə como en *near* /nɪə(r)/
eə como en *hair* /heə(r)/
ʊə como en *pure* /pjʊə(r)/

Consonantes

p como en *pen* /pen/
b como en *ball* /bɔːl/
t como en *toy* /tɔɪ/
d como en *dog* /dɒg/
k como en *cat* /kæt/
g como en *goat* /gəʊt/
tʃ como en *chin* /tʃɪn/
dʒ como en *jaw* /dʒɔː/

f como en *five* /faɪv/
v como en *van* /væn/
θ como en *thin* /θɪn/
ð como en *there* /ðeə(r)/
s como en *sea* /siː/
z como en *zip* /zɪp/
ʃ como en *she* /ʃiː/
ʒ como en *measure* /ˈmeʒə(r)/

h como en *hair* /heə(r)/
m como en *mouse* /maʊs/
n como en *neck* /nek/
ŋ como en *wing* /wɪŋ/
l como en *ball* /bɔːl/
r como en *root* /ruːt/
j como en *year* /jɜː(r)/
w como en *wing* /wɪŋ/

/ˈ/ es el acento *principal* como en *pineapple* /ˈpaɪnæpl/.

/ˌ/ es el acento *secundario* como en *magazine* /ˌmægəˈziːn/.

/(r)/ significa que la /r/ se pronuncia solamente antes de una palabra que empieza por una vocal, por ejemplo *fire* /ˈfaɪə(r)/, *fire-engine* /ˈfaɪər endʒɪn/.

Normalmente aquí los sustantivos se han puesto en su forma *singular*. La mayor parte de ellos hacen el *plural* añadiendo 's' o 'es' si terminan en 's', 'ss', 'ch', 'x', 'sh' o añadiendo 'ies' en lugar de una 'y' final. Hay algunos sustantivos que tienen un plural irregular (foot/feet, man/men, potato/potatoes, scarf/scarves etc.) Si Vd. no sabe cual es el plural de un sustantivo que se encuentra en el índice, consulte su diccionario o su·libro de gramática. Los sustantivos que (generalmente) se usan sólo en la forma *singular* tienen ‡. Los que (generalmente) se usan sólo en el *plural* tienen †. Los sustantivos cuyas formas *singular* y *plural* son idénticas tienen ‡†.

Index

abdomen /ˈæbdəmən/ 59/18
above /əˈbʌv/ 77/1
accelerator /əkˈseləreɪtə(r)/ 38/18; 40/32
accused /əˈkjuːzd/ 16/20
ace /eɪs/ 52/14
acorn /ˈeɪkɔːn/ 63/16
across /əˈkrɒs/ 77/7
actor /ˈæktə(r)/ 50/2
actress /ˈæktrɪs/ 50/3
acute /əˈkjuːt/ 68/11
adding-machine /ˈædɪŋ məʃiːn/ 21/3
address /əˈdres/ 22/11
adjective /ˈædʒɪktɪv/ 74–75
adverb /ˈædvɜːb/ 78
advertisement /ədˈvɜːtɪsmənt/ 15/21
aerial /ˈeərɪəl/ 26/19; 38/9
aeroplane /ˈeərəpleɪn/ 44/9
Africa /ˈæfrɪkə/ 6/4
against /əˈgenst/ 76/8
air /eə(r)/ 44
‡†aircraft /ˈeəkrɑːft/ 44/17
'aircraft-carrier 45/18
Air-Force /ˈeə fɔːs/ 45/C
'airletter 22/7
'airliner 44/9
‡'airmail 22/10
'airport 44
'air-pump 39/9
'air-steward 44/8
aisle /aɪl/ 50/21
alarm-clock /əˈlɑːm klɒk/ 32/24
Alaska /əˈlæskə/ 6/15
along /əˈlɒŋ/ 77/9
Alps /ælps/ 7/38
Amazon /ˈæməzən/ 7/46
ambulance /ˈæmbjʊləns/ 39/15
America /əˈmerɪkə/ 6/1, 2
among /əˈmʌŋ/ 77/5
amplifier' /ˈæmplɪfaɪə(r)/ 49/27

anchor /ˈæŋkə(r)/ 42/11
Andes /ˈændiːz/ 7/37
angle /ˈæŋgl/ 68/10, 11, 14
animal /ˈænɪml/ 56–60
ankle /ˈæŋkl/ 8/36
announcer /əˈnaʊnsə(r)/ 54/15
ant /ænt/ 59/17
Antarctic /ænˈtɑːktɪk/ 5/6; 6/14
Antarctica /ænˈtɑːktɪkə/ 6/7
antelope /ˈæntɪləʊp/ 57/5
antenna /ænˈtenə/ 59/24
antler /ˈæntlə(r)/ 56/12
apex /ˈeɪpeks/ 68/8
apple /ˈæpl/ 61/1
April /ˈeɪprəl/ 80
Arabian Desert /əˌreɪbɪən ˈdezət/ 7/43
Arabian Sea /əˌreɪbɪən ˈsiː/ 6/27
arc /ɑːk/ 68/16
Arctic /ˈɑːktɪk/ 5/2; 6/8
area /ˈeərɪə/ 47/9, 10
arm /ɑːm/ 8/21, 22
'arm'chair 29/8
'armpit 8/20
Army /ˈɑːmɪ/ 45/A
artery /ˈɑːtərɪ/ 9/30
articulated lorry /ɑːˌtɪkjʊleɪtɪd ˈlɒrɪ/ 39/11
artist /ˈɑːtɪst/ 54/8
ash /æʃ/ 51/9
ashtray /ˈæʃtreɪ/ 51/10
Asia /ˈeɪʃə/ 6/5
assistant /əˈsɪstənt/ 20/8
astronaut /ˈæstrənɔːt/ 4/20
at /æt/ 77/8
Atlantic /ətˈlæntɪk/ 6/11, 12
attendant /əˈtendənt/ 39/10
aubergine /ˈəʊbəʒiːn/ 62/16
August /ˈɔːgəst/ 80
aunt /ɑːnt/ 71/10
Australia /ɒˈstreɪlɪə/ 6/6
away /əˈweɪ/ 77/11
axe /æks/ 23/12; 25/7

baboon /bəˈbuːn/ 57/12
baby /ˈbeɪbɪ/ 32/B
back /bæk/ 8/15; 47/15, 16; 69/6
backboard /ˈbækbɔːd/ 46/16
backbone /ˈbækbəʊn/ 8/6
bad /bæd/ 75/8
bag /bæg/ 13/16; 20/6; 35/3; 67/5, 7, 15
†baggage /ˈbægɪdʒ/ 44/4
bail /beɪl/ 48/8
‡†bait /beɪt/ 48/22
baker /ˈbeɪkə(r)/ 55/7
balance /ˈbæləns/ 19/1
balcony /ˈbælkənɪ/ 26/4; 50/10
ball /bɔːl/ 35/26; 46/17; 47/1; 48/10, 28; 73/1
Baltic Sea /ˌbɔːltɪk ˈsiː/ 6/21
banana /bəˈnɑːnə/ 61/5
bandage /ˈbændɪdʒ/ 17/27
banister /ˈbænɪstə(r)/ 28/18
bank-clerk /ˈbæŋk klɑːk/ 54/4
banknote /ˈbæŋknəʊt/ 20/24
bar /bɑː(r)/ 16/16; 51; 73/2, 3
barber /ˈbɑːbə(r)/ 55/6
barge /bɑːdʒ/ 43/16
bark /bɑːk/ 63/17
barmaid /ˈbɑːmeɪd/ 51/17
barman /ˈbɑːmən/ 51/18
barn /bɑːn/ 36/4
barrel /ˈbærəl/ 45/14; 67/4
barrier /ˈbærɪə(r)/ 44/6
barrow /ˈbærəʊ/ 14/4
'bar-stool 51/20
base /beɪs/ 68/9
‡baseball /ˈbeɪsbɔːl/ 48/A
basin /ˈbeɪsn/ 33/11
basket /ˈbɑːskɪt/ 15/30; 20/7; 21/12, 13; 30/23; 33/26; 46/15; 67/10
‡basketball /ˈbɑːskɪtbɔːl/ 46/C
bass /beɪs/ 49/9
bat /bæt/ 46/19; 48/4, 7; 56/25
bath /bɑːθ/ 33/11
bathing-costume /ˈbeɪðɪŋ kɒstjuːm/ 35/36

†**bathing trunks** /'beɪðɪŋ trʌŋks/ 35/20
bathmat /'bɑ:θmæt/ 33/23
bathroom /'bɑ:θrʊm/ 33
baton /'bætən/ 49/11
batsman /'bætsmən/ 48/6
batter /'bætə(r)/ 48/5
battery /'bætərɪ/ 38/32
bay /beɪ/ 5/8; 6/C
bayonet /'beɪənɪt/ 45/3
beach /bi:tʃ/ 35/11
'**beachball** 35/26
beak /bi:k/ 60/4
beaker /'bi:kə(r)/ 19/15
bean /bi:n/ 62/1
bear /beə(r)/ 57/8
beard /bɪəd/ 9/11
beat /bi:t/ 66/5
beautiful /'bju:tɪfl/ 75/9
bed /bed/ 17/19; 27/21; 32/1
bedroom /'bedrʊm/ 32
bedside table /'bedsaɪd 'teɪbl/ 32/9
bedspread /'bedspred/ 32/7
bee /bi:/ 59/21
beehive /'bi:haɪv/ 36/25
beer /bɪə(r)/ 51/1
beetle /'bi:tl/ 59/13
beetroot /'bi:tru:t/ 62/9
behind /bɪ'haɪnd/ 76/16
bell /bel/ 17/9; 28/3; 40/2
below /bɪ'ləʊ/ 76/3
belt /belt/ 13/10; 38/24
bench /bentʃ/ 19/7; 24/1
bend /bend/ 66/4
Bengal (Bay of) /ˌbeŋ'gɔ:l/ 6/28
Bering Sea /ˌbeərɪŋ 'si:/ 7/35
berry /'berɪ/ 63/5
beside /bɪ'saɪd/ 76/14
between /bɪ'twi:n/ 77/12
beyond /bɪ'jɒnd/ 77/2
bib /bɪb/ 32/35
bicycle /'baɪsɪkl/ 14/6; 40/1
big /bɪg/ 74/1
bike /baɪk/ 40/1
bill /bɪl/ 60/19
bin /bɪn/ 15/30; 30/9, 15
bird /bɜ:d/ 60
biscuit /'bɪskɪt/ 20/20
bishop /'bɪʃəp/ 52/6
bit /bɪt/ 25/6; 46/6
black /blæk/ 79
blackbird /'blækbɜ:d/ 60/32
blackboard /'blækbɔ:d/ 18/2
Black Sea /ˌblæk 'si:/ 6/23
bladder /'blædə(r)/ 9/28
blade /bleɪd/ 33/13
blanket /'blæŋkɪt/ 32/6
blind /blaɪnd/ 26/15
blinkers /'blɪŋkəz/ 40/22
block /blɒk/ 15/19, 20
blotter /'blɒtə(r)/ 21/4
blotting-pad /'blɒtɪŋ pæd/ 21/4
blouse /blaʊz/ 13/1
blow /bləʊ/ 64/1
blue /blu:/ 79
blunt /blʌnt/ 74/2
board /bɔ:d/ 29/40; 52/2
boat /bəʊt/ 35/34; 43/6, 12
body /'bɒdɪ/ 8–9
boil /bɔɪl/ 66/22
bollard /'bɒləd/ 42/14
bolt /bəʊlt/ 25/8; 28/8
bomb /bɒm/ 45/24
bomber /'bɒmə(r)/ 45/23
bone /bəʊn/ 8/A
bonnet /'bɒnɪt/ 13/4; 38/26
book /bʊk/ 18/18, 19; 28/29; 30/24; 52/15
bookcase /'bʊkkeɪs/ 29/10
bookshelf /'bʊkʃelf/ 50/25
boot /bu:t/ 10/10; 38/2
bottle /'bɒtl/ 17/30; 32/33; 51/1, 24
bottom /'bɒtəm/ 8/19; 69/2
bough /baʊ/ 63/13
bowl /bəʊl/ 29/39; 73/14
bowler /'bəʊlə(r)/ 48/14
box /bɒks/ 14/1; 15/31; 16/18; 17/29; 22/4; 26/13; 28/5; 32/22, 23; 51/15; 67/19; 73/10
boxer /'bɒksə(r)/ 46/11
‡**boxing** /'bɒksɪŋ/ 46/B
boy /bɔɪ/ 10
bra /brɑ:/ 12/1
brace /breɪs/ 25/5
bracelet /'breɪslɪt/ 12/9
brain /breɪn/ 9/21

brake /breɪk/ 38/19, 22; 40/14, 33
branch /brɑ:ntʃ/ 27/13; 63/13
brassière /'bræsɪə(r)/ 12/1
‡**bread** /bred/ 20/19
break /breɪk/ 64/2
breastbone /'brestbəʊn/ 8/4
†**breeches** /'brɪtʃɪz/ 46/18
brick /brɪk/ 23/8
bricklayer /'brɪkleɪə(r)/ 23/2
bridge /brɪdʒ/ 14/13
bridle /'braɪdl/ 46/5
briefcase /'bri:fkeɪs/ 67/3
brigade /brɪ'geɪd/ 17/A
brooch /brəʊtʃ/ 13/15
broom /bru:m/ 31/2
brother /'brʌðə(r)/ 71/5
brother-in-law /'brʌðər ɪn lɔ:/ 71/8
brow /braʊ/ 9/8
brown /braʊn/ 79
brush /brʌʃ/ 30/27; 31/6, 10; 32/18, 20; 33/14, 15, 18
bucket /'bʌkɪt/ 31/19; 35/24
buckle /'bʌkl/ 13/11
bud /bʌd/ 62/25
budgerigar /'bʌdʒərɪgɑ:(r)/ 60/26
buffalo /'bʌfələʊ/ 56/8
buffer /'bʌfə(r)/ 41/29
building /'bɪldɪŋ/ 23
bulb /bʌlb/ 31/13
bull /bʊl/ 36/23
bullet /'bʊlɪt/ 45/11
bumper /'bʌmpə(r)/ 38/6
bunch /bʌntʃ/ 72/1
bundle /'bʌndl/ 72/2
bungalow /'bʌŋgələʊ/ 35/8
Bunsen burner /ˌbʌnsən 'bɜ:nə(r)/ 19/12
buoy /bɔɪ/ 42/13
bus /bʌs/ 15/26
bush /bʊʃ/ 27/22
'**bus-stop** 15/28
butcher /'bʊtʃə(r)/ 54/2
butter-dish /'bʌtə dɪʃ/ 29/32
butterfly /'bʌtəflaɪ/ 59/25
buttocks /'bʌtəks/ 8/19
button /'bʌtn/ 53/15
'**button-hole** 53/16
by /baɪ/ 76/15

cabbage /'kæbɪdʒ/ 62/11
cabin-cruiser /'kæbɪn kru:zə(r)/ 43/2
cabinet /'kæbɪnɪt/ 29/19; 33/10
cable /'keɪbl/ 22/16; 37/4; 40/4; 42/15
cactus /'kæktəs/ 61/31
cage /keɪdʒ/ 67/14
cake /keɪk/ 20/21
'**cake-tin** 30/19
calculator /'kælkjʊleɪtə(r)/ 21/3
calendar /'kælɪndə(r)/ 18/23; 21/17; 70/11
calf /kɑ:f/ 8/35; 36/22
call-box /'kɔ:l bɒks/ 15/31
calm /kɑ:m/ 75/4
camel /'kæml/ 56/6
camera /'kæmərə/ 52/25
‡**camping** /'kæmpɪŋ/ 35/A
can /kæn/ 27/23; 30/22; 51/4
canal /kə'næl/ 34/1
canary /kə'neərɪ/ 60/18
Cancer /'kænsə(r)/ 5/3
cane /keɪn/ 63/9
canoe /kə'nu:/ 43/8
cap /kæp/ 10/16; 38/3; 46/9
Capricorn /'kæprɪkɔ:n/ 5/5
capsule /'kæpsju:l/ 4/19
captain /'kæptɪn/ 44/5
car /kɑ:(r)/ 15/33; 16/5; 38; 39/16
caravan /'kærəvæn/ 39/13
‡**carbon-paper** /'kɑ:bən peɪpə(r)/ 21/20
card /kɑ:d/ 52/B
cardigan /'kɑ:dɪgən/ 10/13
card-index /'kɑ:d ɪndeks/ 50/23
cargo /'kɑ:gəʊ/ 42/6
Caribbean /ˌkærɪ'bi:ən/ 6/18
'**car-park** 15/32
carpenter /'kɑ:pəntə(r)/ 54/3
carpet /'kɑ:pɪt/ 29/3
carrier-bag /ˌkærɪə 'bæg/ 20/6; 67/15
carrot /'kærət/ 62/5
carry /'kærɪ/ 64/3
cart /kɑ:t/ 40/26
carton /'kɑ:tn/ 67/1
cartridge /'kɑ:trɪdʒ/ 45/11
case /keɪs/ 32/4; 67/17
cash-desk /'kæʃ desk/ 20/4

cashier /'kæʃɪə(r)/ 20/2
cash-register /'kæʃ redʒɪstə(r)/ 20/3
Caspian Sea /ˌkæspɪən 'si:/ 6/24
castle /'kɑ:sl/ 52/4
cat /kæt/ 56/15
catch /kætʃ/ 64/4
catcher /'kætʃə(r)/ 48/1
caterpillar /'kætəpɪlə(r)/ 59/27
cauliflower /'kɒlɪflaʊə(r)/ 62/10
cedar /'si:də(r)/ 63/23
ceiling /'si:lɪŋ/ 29/1
cell /sel/ 16/15
cello /'tʃeləʊ/ 49/8
cement /sɪ'ment/ 23/16
ce'ment-mixer 23/21
centigrade /'sentɪgreɪd/ 70/C
centimetre /'sentɪmi:tə(r)/ 80
centipede /'sentɪpi:d/ 58/22
centre /'sentə(r)/ 47/18, 22; 68/20
century /'sentʃərɪ/ 80
chain /tʃeɪn/ 28/7; 40/18
chair /tʃeə(r)/ 17/15; 29/8, 24; 35/19
chalet /'ʃæleɪ/ 35/8
‡**chalk** /tʃɔ:k/ 18/4
chameleon /kə'mi:lɪən/ 59/3
cheek /tʃi:k/ 9/5
‡**cheese** /tʃi:z/ 20/9
cherry /'tʃerɪ/ 61/7
‡**chess** /tʃes/ 52/A
'**chessmen** 52/1
chest /tʃest/ 8/14
chest-of-drawers /ˌtʃest əv 'drɔ:z/ 32/15
chick /tʃɪk/ 36/35
chicken /'tʃɪkɪn/ 36/33
children /'tʃɪldrən/ 71/2
chimney /'tʃɪmnɪ/ 26/2; 37/7
chin /tʃɪn/ 9/6
China Sea /ˌtʃaɪnə 'si:/ 7/31, 32
chisel /'tʃɪzl/ 24/4
choke /tʃəʊk/ 38/15
chop /tʃɒp/ 66/23
chopper /'tʃɒpə(r)/ 24/15
cigarette /ˌsɪgə'ret/ 51/8
cinema /'sɪnəmə/ 50/17
circle /'sɜ:kl/ 5/2, 6; 50/10; 68/E
circumference /sə'kʌmfərəns/ 68/12
clap /klæp/ 66/17
clarinet /ˌklærɪ'net/ 49/2
claw /klɔ:/ 58/18; 60/3
clean /kli:n/ 74/3
clerk /klɑ:k/ 22/1; 54/4
cliff /klɪf/ 35/6
climb /klaɪm/ 64/5
clip /klɪp/ 21/9
clock /klɒk/ 28/24; 32/24
'**clock-face** 70/4
closed /kləʊzd/ 74/4
cloth /klɒθ/ 30/29, 32; 51/30; 53/13
clothes /kləʊðz/ 10–13; 32/17
cloud /klaʊd/ 27/2
clown /klaʊn/ 64/1
club /klʌb/ 52/11
clutch /klʌtʃ/ 38/20
coach /kəʊtʃ/ 39/17; 41/4
coastline /'kəʊstlaɪn/ 5/11
coat /kəʊt/ 11/14; 13/9
cobweb /'kɒbweb/ 58/26
cock /kɒk/ 36/34
cockpit /'kɒkpɪt/ 45/22
cockroach /'kɒkrəʊtʃ/ 59/14
‡**cocoa** /'kəʊkəʊ/ 63/4
coconut /'kəʊkənʌt/ 61/9
cocoon /kə'ku:n/ 59/28
‡**coffee** /'kɒfɪ/ 63/5
cog /kɒg/ 40/19
coil /kɔɪl/ 59/7
coin /kɔɪn/ 20/25
colander /'kʌləndə(r)/ 30/25
cold /kəʊld/ 33/3; 74/15
collar /'kɒlə(r)/ 11/2
'**collar-bone** 8/2
collector /kə'lektə(r)/ 41/16
colour /'kʌlə(r)/ 79
comb /kəʊm/ 32/21; 66/12
combine harvester /ˌkɒmbaɪn 'hɑ:vɪstə(r)/ 36/16
comet /'kɒmɪt/ 4/1
compact /'kɒmpækt/ 12/13
compartment /kəm'pɑ:tmənt/ 41/5
compass /'kʌmpəs/ 5/C
†**compasses** /'kɒmpəsɪz/ 18/11
concrete-mixer /'kɒnkri:t mɪksə(r)/ 23/21
conductor /kən'dʌktə(r)/ 15/27; 49/10

cone /kəʊn/ 63/21; 68/23
Congo /'kɒŋgəʊ/ 7/50
consonant /'kɒnsənənt/ 81
constellation /ˌkɒnstə'leɪʃn/ 4/2
container /kən'teɪnə(r)/ 67
continent /'kɒntɪnənt/ 6/A
control-panel /kən'trəʊl pænl/ 45/28
control tower /kən'trəʊl taʊə(r)/ 44/20
convertible /kən'vɜːtəbl/ 38/38
cooker /'kʊkə(r)/ 30/1
cookery-book /'kʊkəri bʊk/ 30/24
cooling tower /'kuːlɪŋ taʊə(r)/ 37/8
Coral Sea /ˌkɒrəl 'siː/ 6/29
cord /kɔːd/ 28/28
core /kɔː(r)/ 61/4
cork /kɔːk/ 51/25
corkscrew /'kɔːkskruː/ 51/11
corn /kɔːn/ 63/10
corner /'kɔːnə(r)/ 69/3
cot /kɒt/ 32/26
‡cotton /'kɒtn/ 53/8; 63/6; 73/9
couch /kaʊtʃ/ 29/21
counter /'kaʊntə(r)/ 20/22; 22/3; 50/24
country /'kʌntri/ 34
coupé /'kuːpeɪ/ 38/39
court /kɔːt/ 16/C; 48/23
cousin /'kʌzn/ 71/9
cover /'kʌvə(r)/ 52/16
cow /kaʊ/ 36/21
'cowshed 36/3
crab /kræb/ 58/17
crane /kreɪn/ 23/1; 42/4
crash-helmet /'kræʃ helmɪt/ 40/27
crate /kreɪt/ 67/11
crawl /krɔːl/ 64/6
cream /kriːm/ 12/18
crease /kriːs/ 48/17
crescent /'kresnt/ 4/11
crest /krest/ 60/12
‡cricket /'krɪkɪt/ 48/B; 59/11
crocodile /'krɒkədaɪl/ 59/1
crook /krʊk/ 36/27
crooked /'krʊkɪd/ 74/5
crutch /krʌtʃ/ 17/26
cry /kraɪ/ 64/7
crystal /'krɪstl/ 19/17
cube /kjuːb/ 68/24
cucumber /'kjuːkʌmbə(r)/ 62/8
cuff /kʌf/ 11/3
cup /kʌp/ 29/30
cupboard /'kʌbəd/ 32/13
curtain /'kɜːtn/ 26/14; 29/7; 50/6
curve /kɜːv/ 68/3
cushion /'kʊʃn/ 29/9
customer /'kʌstəmə(r)/ 20/5; 51/22
†customs /'kʌstəmz/ 44/1, 2
'customs-officer 44/2
cut /kʌt/ 64/8
cycle /'saɪkl/ 40/1
cylinder /'sɪlɪndə(r)/ 68/25
'cylinder-head 38/36
†cymbals /'sɪmblz/ 49/29

daffodil /'dæfədɪl/ 62/17
daisy /'deɪzi/ 62/18
dam /dæm/ 37/2
dance /dɑːns/ 64/9
Danube /'dænjuːb/ 7/47
dark /dɑːk/ 75/11
dashboard /'dæʃbɔːd/ 38/12
date /deɪt/ 61/10; 70/B
daughter /'dɔːtə(r)/ 71/3
daughter-in-law /'dɔːtər ɪn lɔː/ 71/7
day /deɪ/ 80
December /dɪ'sembə(r)/ 80
decimal /'desɪml/ 69/21
deck /dek/ 43/19
'deckchair 35/19
deep /diːp/ 74/6
ˌdeep-'freeze 20/14
defence /dɪ'fens/ 45
defendant /dɪ'fendənt/ 16/20
defender /dɪ'fendə(r)/ 47/15, 16
degree /dɪ'griː/ 70/C
delta /'deltə/ 5/9
dental nurse /'dentl nɜːs/ 17/14
dentist /'dentɪst/ 17/16
depth /depθ/ 69/10
derrick /'derɪk/ 37/10
desert /'dezət/ 7/E
desk /desk/ 18/7; 21/1; 50/24
‡detection /dɪ'tekʃn/ 16/A/15
diagonal /daɪ'ægənl/ 68/25

dial /'daɪəl/ 19/5; 28/27
diameter /daɪ'æmɪtə(r)/ 68/19
diamond /'daɪəmənd/ 52/12
diary /'daɪəri/ 21/5
difficult /'dɪfɪkəlt/ 74/12
dig /dɪg/ 64/10
dining-table /'daɪnɪŋ teɪbl/ 29/23
diphthong /'dɪfθɒŋ/ 81
directory /dɪ'rektəri/ 28/29
dirty /'dɜːti/ 74/3
dish /dɪʃ/ 29/32
'dish-cloth 30/29
distributor /dɪ'strɪbjʊtə(r)/ 38/34
dive /daɪv/ 64/11
divide by /dɪ'vaɪd baɪ/ 69/18
dock /dɒk/ 16/21; 42/12
docker /'dɒkə(r)/ 54/6
doctor /'dɒktə(r)/ 17/21; 55/8
dog /dɒg/ 16/6; 36/28; 56/13
doll /dɒl/ 32/31
dolphin /'dɒlfɪn/ 57/3
donkey /'dɒŋki/ 56/10
door /dɔː(r)/ 26/7; 28/1
'doorstep 28/4
double bass /ˌdʌbl 'beɪs/ 49/9
dove /dʌv/ 60/24
down /daʊn/ 76/4
ˌdown'stairs 28/21
dragonfly /'drægənflaɪ/ 59/19
drain /dreɪn/ 14/11
draining-board /'dreɪnɪŋ bɔːd/ 30/8
'drainpipe 26/17
†draughts /drɑːfts/ 52/9
draw /drɔː/ 64/12
drawer /drɔː(r)/ 32/15
dream /driːm/ 64/14
dress /dres/ 13/8
dressing-gown /'dresɪŋ gaʊn/ 10/3
dressing-table /'dresɪŋ teɪbl/ 32/10
dressmaker /'dresmeɪkə(r)/ 54/10
drill /drɪl/ 17/17; 23/23; 25/3, 4
drink /drɪŋk/ 51/13; 64/13
drive /draɪv/ 64/15
driver /'draɪvə(r)/ 41/2; 54/12
drown /draʊn/ 64/16
drum /drʌm/ 49/30
dry /draɪ/ 74/7
ˌdrying-'up cloth 30/32
duck /dʌk/ 36/32
duckling /'dʌklɪŋ/ 36/31
dummy /'dʌmi/ 32/28
dumper-truck /'dʌmpə trʌk/ 23/22
dustbin /'dʌstbɪn/ 67/8
duster /'dʌstə(r)/ 18/5; 31/7
dust-jacket /'dʌst dʒækɪt/ 52/17
dustpan /'dʌstpæn/ 31/8

eagle /'iːgl/ 60/2
ear /ɪə(r)/ 9/3; 63/2
'ear-ring 12/10
‡Earth /ɜːθ/ 4/7
easel /'iːzl/ 18/3
east /iːst/ 5/C
ˌEast 'China 'Sea 7/32
easy /'iːzi/ 74/12
eat /iːt/ 64/17
eclipse /ɪ'klɪps/ 4/10
edge /edʒ/ 69/4
‡education /ˌedjuː'keɪʃn/ 18–19
eel /iːl/ 58/10
egg /eg/ 20/11
'eggplant 62/16
eight /eɪt/ 80
eighteen /ˌeɪ'tiːn/ 80
eighth /eɪtθ/ 80
eighty /'eɪti/ 80
‡elastic /ɪ'læstɪk/ 53/7
elbow /'elbəʊ/ 8/23
electric /ɪ'lektrɪk/ 25/4; 49/26
electrician /ˌɪlek'trɪʃn/ 55/2
elephant /'elɪfənt/ 57/21
eleven /ɪ'levn/ 80
ellipse /ɪ'lɪps/ 68/F
empty /'empti/ 74/8
engine /'endʒɪn/ 17/7; 38/31; 41/3; 44/12
envelope /'envələʊp/ 21/11; 22/14
equal /'iːkwəl/ 69/19
Equator /ɪ'kweɪtə(r)/ 5/4
escape /ɪ'skeɪp/ 17/10
estate /ɪ'steɪt/ 38/40
estuary /'estjʊəri/ 5/10
Europe /'jʊərəp/ 6/3
excavator /'ekskəveɪtə(r)/ 23/20
exercise-book /'eksəsaɪz bʊk/ 18/18

exhaust(-pipe) /ɪg'zɔːst paɪp/ 38/7; 40/35
extinguisher /ɪk'stɪŋgwɪʃə(r)/ 17/6
eye /aɪ/ 9/1; 9/D; 53/23
'eyeball 9/15
'eyebrow 9/16
'eyelash 9/18
'eyelid 9/17
‡'eye-shadow 12/17

face /feɪs/ 9/C; 70/4
‡'face-cream 12/18
('face-)flannel 33/17
Fahrenheit /'færənhaɪt/ 70/C
fall /fɔːl/ 64/18
family /'fæməli/ 71
fan /fæn/ 21/14
farm /fɑːm/ 36
farmer /'fɑːmə(r)/ 36/15
'farmhouse 36/7
'farmyard 36/6
fast /fɑːst/ 74/9
fastener /'fɑːsnə(r)/ 53/22
fat /fæt/ 74/10
father /'fɑːðə(r)/ 71/4
father-in-law /'fɑːðər ɪn lɔː/ 71/6
feather /'feðə(r)/ 60/5
February /'febrʊəri/ 80
feeler /'fiːlə(r)/ 59/16
fence /fens/ 36/10
fern /fɜːn/ 61/32
ferry /'feri/ 43/15
field /fiːld/ 34/13; 36/8; 47/6
fielder /'fiːldə(r)/ 48/15
fifteen /ˌfɪf'tiːn/ 80
fifth /fɪfθ/ 80
fifty /'fɪfti/ 80
fig /fɪg/ 61/29
fight /faɪt/ 64/19
fighter plane /'faɪtə pleɪn/ 45/21
figure /'fɪgə(r)/ 68/G
file /faɪl/ 12/12; 21/18; 24/2
filing-cabinet /'faɪlɪŋ kæbɪnət/ 21/19
film /fɪlm/ 52/24
fin /fɪn/ 44/13; 57/4; 58/2
finger /'fɪŋgə(r)/ 8/30
'fingerprint 16/11
fir /fɜː(r)/ 63/20
fire /'faɪə(r)/ 17/11; 29/6
'fire brigade 17/A
'fire-engine 17/7
'fire-escape 17/10
'fire-extinguisher 17/6
'fireman 17/1
'fireplace 29/4
first /fɜːst/ 75/10; 80
fish /fɪʃ/ 58
fisherman /'fɪʃəmən/ 48/18
fishing /'fɪʃɪŋ/ 48/C
fist /fɪst/ 8/26
five /faɪv/ 80
flag /flæg/ 41/11
flame /fleɪm/ 17/13
flamingo /flə'mɪŋgəʊ/ 60/8
flannel /'flænl/ 33/17
flap /flæp/ 22/15
flask /flɑːsk/ 19/16; 67/9
flat /flæt/ 15/19
fleet /fliːt/ 72/4
‡flex /fleks/ 31/12
flight /flaɪt/ 72/5
flipper /'flɪpə(r)/ 35/21; 57/10
flock /flɒk/ 72/6
floor /flɔː(r)/ 28/11
florist /'flɒrɪst/ 55/5
flower /'flaʊə(r)/ 27/20; 62
'flower-bed 27/1
'flower-pot 27/24
fluke /fluːk/ 57/2
flute /fluːt/ 49/1
fly /flaɪ/ 59/23; 64/20
'fly-over 39/2
foal /fəʊl/ 56/2
foot /fʊt/ 8/37; 60/9
‡'football 47/A
'footbrake 38/19
‡'footlights 50/13
'footpath 34/17
'footprint 16/12
'footrest 40/37
forearm /'fɔːrɑːm/ 8/24
forehead /'fɒrɪd/ 9/8
forest /'fɒrɪst/ 34/9
fork /fɔːk/ 24/10; 27/25; 29/26
ˌfork-lift 'truck 42/17

forty /ˈfɔːtɪ/ 80
forward /ˈfɔːwəd/ 47/22
†foundations /faʊnˈdeɪʃnz/ 23/10
four /fɔː(r)/ 80
fourteen /ˌfɔːˈtiːn/ 80
fourth /fɔːθ/ 80
fox /fɒks/ 56/24
fraction /ˈfrækʃn/ 69/22
frame /freɪm/ 26/9; 29/13
freezer /ˈfriːzə(r)/ 20/14
Friday /ˈfraɪdɪ/ 80
fridge /frɪdʒ/ 30/5
frill /frɪl/ 53/14
frog /frɒg/ 58/20
from /frɒm/ 77/3, 11
frond /frɒnd/ 61/33
front /frʌnt/ 69/7; 76/7
front door 26/7
frown /fraʊn/ 66/14
‡fruit /fruːt/ 20/17; 61
fruit-tree 36/11
frying-pan /ˈfraɪɪŋ pæn/ 30/11
‡fuel /ˈfjʊəl/ 37/9
full /fʊl/ 4/13; 74/8
funnel /ˈfʌnl/ 42/9; 43/21
furrow /ˈfʌrəʊ/ 36/20
fuselage /ˈfjuːzəlɑːʒ/ 44/10

galaxy /ˈgæləksɪ/ 4/3
gallery /ˈgælərɪ/ 50/9
gang /gæŋ/ 72/7
Ganges /ˈgændʒiːz/ 7/52
gangway /ˈgæŋweɪ/ 42/10; 50/21
gaol /dʒeɪl/ 16/B
garage /ˈgærɑːdʒ/ 26/6
garden /ˈgɑːdn/ 24/10; 26/20; 27
gardener /ˈgɑːdnə(r)/ 55/3
gate /geɪt/ 27/16
gauge /geɪdʒ/ 38/13
gear-lever /ˈgɪə liːvə(r)/ 38/21; 40/38
gill /gɪl/ 58/5
giraffe /dʒɪˈrɑːf/ 57/15
girl /gɜːl/ 12
give /gɪv/ 66/11
glass /glɑːs/ 29/29; 51/26
†glasses /ˈglɑːsɪz/ 11/23
glider /ˈglaɪdə(r)/ 44/14
globe /gləʊb/ 5/A
glove /glʌv/ 11/20; 46/12; 48/3
‡glue /gluː/ 18/13
goal /gəʊl/ 46/25; 47/7, 8, 9
goalkeeper 47/14
goal-line 47/8
goat /gəʊt/ 36/24
Gobi /ˈgəʊbɪ/ 7/44
†goggles /ˈgɒglz/ 35/15; 40/28
good /gʊd/ 75/8
goods-truck 41/28
goose /guːs/ 60/25
gorilla /gəˈrɪlə/ 57/14
gown /gaʊn/ 16/24
gram /græm/ 80
granddaughter /ˈgrændˌdɔːtə(r)/ 71/12
grandson /ˈgrænsʌn/ 71/12
grape /greɪp/ 61/12
‡†grapefruit /ˈgreɪpfruːt/ 61/30
grass /grɑːs/ 26/21
grasshopper /ˈgrɑːshɒpə(r)/ 59/12
green /griːn/ 79
greengrocer /ˈgriːngrəʊsə(r)/ 55/1
grenade /grɪˈneɪd/ 45/9
grey /greɪ/ 79
grill /grɪl/ 30/3; 38/27
groundnut /ˈgraʊndnʌt/ 61/11
groundsheet /ˈgraʊndʃiːt/ 35/2
guard /gɑːd/ 41/10
guided missile /ˌgaɪdɪd ˈmɪsaɪl/ 45/4
Guinea (Gulf of) /ˈgɪnɪ/ 6/19
guitar /gɪˈtɑː(r)/ 49/26
gulf /gʌlf/ 6/C
gull /gʌl/ 60/21
gum /gʌm/ 18/13
gun /gʌn/ 45/6, 15
gutter /ˈgʌtə(r)/ 14/10; 26/16
gym-shoe /ˈdʒɪm ʃuː/ 10/15

hacksaw /ˈhæksɔː/ 25/18
hair /heə(r)/ 8/9
hairbrush 32/20
hairdresser 54/1
hairdrier 31/14
half /hɑːf/ 4/12; 47/17, 18, 19; 69/12
halfway line 43/13
hall /hɔːl/ 28; 44/1

hammer /ˈhæmə(r)/ 25/14
hand /hænd/ 8/27; 70/1, 2, 3
handbag 13/16; 67/5
handbrake 38/22
†handcuffs 16/8
hand-drill 25/3
hand-grenade 45/9
handkerchief /ˈhæŋkətʃɪf/ 13/14
handle /ˈhændl/ 25/16; 29/38; 33/8
†handle-bars 40/6
handrail 28/19
hangar /ˈhæŋə(r)/ 44/21
hanger /ˈhæŋə(r)/ 32/19
happy /ˈhæpɪ/ 74/11
hard /hɑːd/ 74/12, 13
‡harness /ˈhɑːnɪs/ 40/23
hat /hæt/ 11/13; 13/4
hawk /hɔːk/ 60/6
hay /heɪ/ 36/2
hayloft 36/1
he /hiː/ 79
head /hed/ 8/10; 25/15
headboard 32/2
headlamp 40/5
headlight 38/29
heap /hiːp/ 72/9
heart /hɑːt/ 9/23; 52/13
heavy /ˈhevɪ/ 75/12
hedge /hedʒ/ 27/17; 34/14
hedgehog /ˈhedʒhɒg/ 56/26
heel /hiːl/ 9/38; 11/11
height /haɪt/ 69/9
helicopter /ˈhelɪkɒptə(r)/ 44/15
helmet /ˈhelmɪt/ 16/2; 17/2; 40/27
hem /hem/ 53/4
hen /hen/ 36/33
her /hɜː(r)/ 79
herd /hɜːd/ 72/10
here /hɪə(r)/ 79
heron /ˈherən/ 60/15
herring /ˈherɪŋ/ 58/6
hers /hɜːz/ 79
†hibiscus /hɪˈbɪskəs/ 62/24
high /haɪ/ 74/14
hill /hɪl/ 34/10
him /hɪm/ 79
Himalayas /ˌhɪməˈleɪəz/ 7/40
hinge /hɪndʒ/ 28/9
hip /hɪp/ 8/18
hip-bone 8/7
hippopotamus /ˌhɪpəˈpɒtəməs/ 57/20
his /hɪz/ 79
hit /hɪt/ 66/5
hobby /ˈhɒbɪ/ 52
‡hockey /ˈhɒkɪ/ 46/D
hod /hɒd/ 23/18
hold /həʊld/ 42/8; 66/20
holdall /ˈhəʊldɔːl/ 67/18
hole /həʊl/ 33/5; 53/16
hole-punch 21/6
hollow /ˈhɒləʊ/ 75/14
hook /hʊk/ 48/21; 53/23
hoover /ˈhuːvə(r)/ 31/1
horizon /həˈraɪzn/ 42/1
horn /hɔːn/ 49/14; 56/9; 57/26
horse /hɔːs/ 40/21; 46/2; 56/1
‡horse-racing 46/A
hosepipe /ˈhəʊzpaɪp/ 17/3
hospital /ˈhɒspɪtl/ 17/C
hot /hɒt/ 33/2; 74/15
hotel /həʊˈtel/ 35/7
hour /ˈaʊə(r)/ 70/2; 80
house /haʊs/ 26; 37/3
household 31
‡†hovercraft /ˈhɒvəkrɑːft/ 42/18
hubcap /ˈhʌbkæp/ 38/30
Hudson Bay /ˌhʌdsn ˈbeɪ/ 6/16
hug /hʌg/ 66/6
human /ˈhjuːmən/ 8-9
humming-bird /ˈhʌmɪŋ bɜːd/ 60/27
hump /hʌmp/ 56/7
hundred /ˈhʌndrəd/ 80
husband /ˈhʌzbənd/ 71/1
Huang He /hwæŋ/ 7/54
hydrant /ˈhaɪdrənt/ 17/5
hypotenuse /haɪˈpɒtənjuːz/ 68/12

I /aɪ/ 79
ice-cream /ˌaɪs ˈkriːm/ 35/17
icicle /ˈaɪsɪkl/ 27/8
†ignition /ɪgˈnɪʃn/ 38/14
illustration /ˌɪləˈstreɪʃn/ 52/20
in /ɪn/ 76/7, 10
index /ˈɪndeks/ 50/23

Indian /ˈɪndɪən/ 6/13
indicator /ˈɪndɪkeɪtə(r)/ 38/5
Indus /ˈɪndəs/ 71/51
insect /ˈɪnsekt/ 59/B
inside /ˌɪnˈsaɪd/ 47/21, 23; 76/10
inside lane 39/6
insides /ˌɪnˈsaɪdz/ 9/E
inspector /ɪnˈspektə(r)/ 41/6
instep /ˈɪnstep/ 9/39
intestines /ɪnˈtestɪnz/ 9/27
into /ˈɪntʊ/ 76/9
iris /ˈaɪərɪs/ 9/20
iron /ˈaɪən/ 31/11; 66/18
ironing-board /ˈaɪənɪŋ bɔːd/ 31/3
‡irrigation /ɪrɪˈgeɪʃn/ 36/17
island /ˈaɪlənd/ 5/12
it /ɪt/ 79
its /ɪts/ 79

jack /dʒæk/ 52/11
jacket /ˈdʒækɪt/ 10/8; 52/17
jail /dʒeɪl/ 16/B
January /ˈdʒænjʊərɪ/ 80
Japan (Sea of) /dʒəˈpæn/ 7/33
jaw /dʒɔː/ 9/9
†jeans /dʒiːnz/ 10/7
jeep dʒiːp/ 45/5
jelly-fish /ˈdʒelɪ fɪʃ/ 58/11
jersey /ˈdʒɜːzɪ/ 13/5
jet /dʒet/ 44/1
‡jewellery /ˈdʒuːəlrɪ/ 32/23
jockey /ˈdʒɒkɪ/ 46/1
†jodhpurs /ˈdʒɒdpəz/ 46/8
joint /ˈdʒɔɪnt/ 73/4
judge /dʒʌdʒ/ 16/22
‡judo /ˈdʒuːdəʊ/ 46/G
judo suit 46/23
jug /dʒʌg/ 29/37; 30/20
juke-box /ˈdʒuːk bɒks/ 51/15
July /dʒuːˈlaɪ/ 80
jump /dʒʌmp/ 64/21
jumper /ˈdʒʌmpə(r)/ 10/6; 13/5
June /dʒuːn/ 80
junk /dʒʌŋk/ 43/5
jury /ˈdʒʊərɪ/ 16/17

Kalahari /kæləˈhɑːrɪ/ 7/42
kangaroo /ˌkæŋgəˈruː/ 57/6
keeper /ˈkiːpə(r)/ 47/14; 48/11
kerb /kɜːb/ 14/9
kernel /ˈkɜːnl/ 61/28
kettle /ˈketl/ 30/13
key /kiː/ 28/15; 49/16
keyhole /ˈkiːhəʊl/ 28/6
kick /kɪk/ 64/22
kidney /ˈkɪdnɪ/ 9/26
kilogram /ˈkɪləgræm/ 80
kilometre /ˈkɪləmiːtə(r)/ 80
king /kɪŋ/ 52/8, 13
kingfisher /ˈkɪŋfɪʃə(r)/ 60/30
kiss /kɪs/ 66/7
kitchen /ˈkɪtʃɪn/ 30
kitten /ˈkɪtn/ 56/16
knave /neɪv/ 52/11
knee /niː/ 8/34
kneecap /ˈniːkæp/ 8/8
kneel /niːl/ 64/23
knife /naɪf/ 24/5; 29/28, 41
knight /naɪt/ 52/5
knitting /ˈnɪtɪŋ/ 53/21
knitting-needle 53/18
knocker /ˈnɒkə(r)/ 28/2

lab /læb/ 19
label /ˈleɪbl/ 22/22
laboratory /ləˈbɒrətrɪ/ 19
‡lace /leɪs/ 53/9
ladder /ˈlædə(r)/ 17/8; 23/5
ladle /ˈleɪdl/ 30/31
lake /leɪk/ 5/13; 34/5
lamb /læm/ 36/30
lamp /læmp/ 29/15; 32/25
lamp-post 15/24
lamp-shade 29/16
lane /leɪn/ 39/5, 6
lapel /ləˈpel/ 11/15
larder /ˈlɑːdə(r)/ 30/6
large /lɑːdʒ/ 74/1
last /lɑːst/ 75/10
latitude /ˈlætɪtjuːd/ 5/15
laugh /lɑːf/ 64/24
launch /lɔːntʃ/ 43/12
launching-pad /ˈlɔːntʃɪŋ pæd/ 4/17

laundry-basket /'lɔːndrɪ bɑːskɪt/ 33/26
lavatory /'lævətrɪ/ 33/7
law /lɔː/ 16
'law court 16/C
lawn /lɔːn/ 27/19
lawyer /'lɔːjə(r)/ 16/23
leaf /liːf/ 63/15
leap /liːp/ 64/21
leaves /liːvz/ 27/15
ledge /ledʒ/ 26/11
left /left/ 47/15, 17, 20, 21
leg /leg/ 8/32
‡leisure /'leʒə(r)/ 50
lemon /'lemən/ 61/14
length /leŋθ/ 69/11; 80
lens /lenz/ 19/10; 52/26
leopard /'lepəd/ 57/18
letter /'letə(r)/ 22/7, 10
'letter-basket 21/12
'letter-box 14/1; 22/4; 28/5
lettuce /'letɪs/ 62/12
librarian /laɪ'breərɪən/ 50/22
library /'laɪbrərɪ/ 50/C
lick /lɪk/ 64/25
lid /lɪd/ 29/35
lie /laɪ/ 65/3
light /laɪt/ 14/7; 17/18; 28/22; 38/4, 5, 29; 40/30; 44/17; 75/11, 12
'light-bulb 31/13
‡lightning /'laɪtnɪŋ/ 27/1
'light-switch 28/13
line /laɪn/ 5/14, 15; 27/28; 47/8, 12, 13; 48/20, 26; 68/A; 73/5
liner /'laɪnə(r)/ 43/20
linesman /'laɪnzmən/ 47/2
'line-up 47/C
lion /'laɪən/ 57/16
lip /lɪp/ 9/13
'lipstick 12/19
liquid /'lɪkwɪd/ 30/28; 80
listen /'lɪsn/ 65/1
litre /'liːtə(r)/ 80
litter-bin/-basket /'lɪtə(r)/ 15/30
little /'lɪtl/ 74/1
liver /'lɪvə(r)/ 9/25
living-room /'lɪvɪŋ rʊm/ 29
lizard /'lɪzəd/ 59/9
llama /'lɑːmə/ 56/5
loaf /ləʊf/ 73/6
lobster /'lɒbstə(r)/ 58/12
lock /lɒk/ 28/7
locust /'ləʊkəst/ 59/10
log /lɒg/ 63/18
long /lɒŋ/ 74/16
longitude /'lɒndʒɪtjuːd/ 5/14
loo /luː/ 33/7
loose /luːs/ 75/16
lorry /'lɒrɪ/ 14/15; 39/14
loud /laʊd/ 75/13
loudspeaker /,laʊd'spiːkə(r)/ 49/28
low /ləʊ/ 74/14
‡luggage /'lʌgɪdʒ/ 44/4
'luggage-rack 41/9
lump /lʌmp/ 73/7
lung /lʌŋ/ 9/24
lychee /,laɪ'tʃiː/ 61/26

mac /mæk/ 11/12
machine /mə'ʃiːn/ 31/4; 53/1
ma'chine-gun 45/15
mackintosh /'mækɪntɒʃ/ 11/12
magnet /'mægnɪt/ 19/19
magnifying-glass /'mægnɪfaɪŋ glɑːs/ 16/10
mailbag /'meɪlbæg/ 22/6
‡maize /meɪz/ 63/1
mallet /'mælɪt/ 25/1
man /mæn/ 10–11
mane /meɪn/ 57/17
mango /'mæŋgəʊ/ 61/15
mantelpiece /'mæntlpiːs/ 29/5
mantis /'mæntɪs/ 59/15
map /mæp/ 5/B; 18/21
March /mɑːtʃ/ 80
market /'mɑːkɪt/ 14/3
marrow /'mærəʊ/ 62/7
‡mascara /mæ'skɑːrə/ 12/14
mask /mɑːsk/ 35/15; 48/2
mast /mɑːst/ 43/3
mat /mæt/ 26/18; 28/10; 29/25; 33/23
match /mætʃ/ 51/16
'matchbox 51/5
material /mə'tɪərɪəl/ 53/13
mattock /'mætək/ 23/19

mattress /'mætrɪs/ 32/8
May /meɪ/ 80
me /miː/ 79
meadow /'medəʊ/ 34/11
measure /'meʒə(r)/ 53/25; 80
measurement /'meʒəmənt/ 69
‡meat /miːt/ 20/13
mechanic /mɪ'kænɪk/ 54/5
medical /'medɪkl/ 17
medicine /'medsɪn/ 17/30
Mediterranean /,medɪtə'reɪnɪən/ 6/22
Mekong /'miːkɒŋ/ 7/53
menu /'menjuː/ 51/23
meter /'miːtə(r)/ 19/4
metre /'miːtə(r)/ 80
Mexico (Gulf of) /'meksɪkəʊ/ 6/17
microphone /'maɪkrəfəʊn/ 49/25
microscope /'maɪkrəskəʊp/ 19/9
midfield /'mɪdfiːld/ 47/17, 18, 19
mike /maɪk/ 49/25
milk /mɪlk/ 20/10
'milk-jug 29/37
millilitre /'mɪlɪliːtə(r)/ 80
millimetre /'mɪlɪmiːtə(r)/ 80
million /'mɪlɪən/ 80
mine /maɪn/ 79
miner /'maɪnə(r)/ 54/7
minus /'maɪnəs/ 69/17
minute /'mɪnɪt/ 70/1; 80
mirror /'mɪrə(r)/ 32/12; 38/1; 40/3
missile /'mɪsaɪl/ 45/4
Mississippi /,mɪsɪ'sɪpɪ/ 7/45
mixer /'mɪksə(r)/ 23/21
Monday /'mʌndɪ/ 80
monkey /'mʌŋkɪ/ 57/13
month /mʌnθ/ 80
Moon /muːn/ 4/6
mop /mɒp/ 31/5
mortar /'mɔːtə(r)/ 19/21
mosquito /mə'skiːtəʊ/ 59/20
moth /mɒθ/ 59/26
mother /'mʌðə(r)/ 71/4
mother-in-law /'mʌðər ɪn lɔː/ 71/6
motor /'məʊtə(r)/ 43/13
'motorbike/motorcycle 14/17; 39/20
'motor-boat 35/34; 43/12
'motor-car 38
'motor-launch 43/12
'motorway 39/1
mountain /'maʊntɪn/ 34/2
'mountain 'range 7
mouse /maʊs/ 56/18
moustache /mə'stɑːʃ/ 9/10
mouth /maʊθ/ 9/4; 58/8
'mouthpiece 49/23
mudguard /'mʌdgɑːd/ 40/10
mug /mʌg/ 51/3
multiply by /'mʌltɪplaɪ/ 69/16
muscle /'mʌsl/ 9/31
mushroom /'mʌʃrʊm/ 62/14
‡music /'mjuːzɪk/ 49
musician /mjuː'zɪʃn/ 49/3
‡mustard /'mʌstəd/ 51/28
my /maɪ/ 79

nail /neɪl/ 8/31; 25/11
'nail-file 12/12
'nailbrush 33/18
‡'nail-polish 12/15
‡'nail-varnish 12/15
napkin /'næpkɪn/ 51/31
nappy /'næpɪ/ 32/36
narrow /'nærəʊ/ 75/1
national /'næʃənl/ 45
navigator /'nævɪgeɪtə(r)/ 45/26
Navy /'neɪvɪ/ 45/B
near /nɪə(r)/ 76/15
neck /nek/ 8/11
necklace /'neklɪs/ 12/11
needle /'niːdl/ 5/16; 19/6; 53/6, 18; 63/22
negative /'negətɪv/ 52/23
nephew /'nevjuː/ 71/11
nest /nest/ 60/29
net /net/ 46/20; 48/24
new /njuː/ 4/11; 75/3
,new 'moon 4/11
next /nekst/ 76/14
niece /niːs/ 71/11
Niger /'naɪdʒə(r)/ 7/49
nightdress /'naɪtdres/ 12/6
'nightgown 12/6
Nile /naɪl/ 7/48
nine /naɪn/ 80

nineteen /naɪn'tiːn/ 80
ninety /'naɪntɪ/ 80
ninth /naɪnθ/ 80
north /nɔːθ/ 5/C
northeast /,nɔːθ'iːst/ 5/C
,North 'Pole 5/1
,North 'Sea 6/20
northwest /,nɔːθ'west/ 5/C
nose /nəʊz/ 9/2
nosecone /'nəʊzkəʊn/ 4/15
note /nəʊt/ 20/24
'notebook 21/23
'notepad 21/23
nothing /'nʌθɪŋ/ 80
noun /naʊn/ 72-73
nought /nɔːt/ 80
November /nəʊ'vembə(r)/ 80
nozzle /'nɒzl/ 17/4
number /'nʌmbə(r)/ 41/21; 80
'number-plate 38/28
nurse /nɜːs/ 17/14, 25; 55/10
nut /nʌt/ 25/13; 61/11, 27

oak /əʊk/ 63/10
oar /ɔː(r)/ 43/7
object /'ɒbdʒɪkt/ 31
oblong /'ɒblɒŋ/ 68/D
obtuse /əb'tjuːs/ 68/10
occupation /,ɒkjʊ'peɪʃn/ 54–55
ocean /'əʊʃn/ 6/B
o'clock /ə'klɒk/ 70/5
October /ɒk'təʊbə(r)/ 80
octopus /'ɒktəpəs/ 58/23
off /ɒf/ 77/6
office /'ɒfɪs/ 21; 41/14
'office-block 15/20
oil-derrick /'ɔɪl derɪk/ 37/10
oil-rig /'ɔɪl rɪg/ 37/11
oil-tanker /'ɔɪl tæŋkə(r)/ 43/18
Okhotsk (Sea of) /əʊ'kɒtsk/ 7/34
old /əʊld/ 4/14; 75/2, 3
olive /'ɒlɪv/ 63/3
on /ɒn/ 76/12
one /wʌn/ 79–80
onion /'ʌnjən/ 62/13
onto /'ɒntʊ/ 76/13
open /'əʊpən/ 65/2; 74/4
opener /'əʊpnə(r)/ 51/7
operator /'ɒpəreɪtə(r)/ 21/16
optician /ɒp'tɪʃn/ 55/14
orange /'ɒrɪndʒ/ 61/16; 79
orbit /'ɔːbɪt/ 4/9
orchard /'ɔːtʃəd/ 36/12
orchestra /'ɔːkɪstrə/ 49; 50/12
orchid /'ɔːkɪd/ 62/21
ostrich /'ɒstrɪtʃ/ 60/1
our /'aʊə(r)/ 79
ours /'aʊəz/ 79
out /aʊt/ 76/11
outboard motor /,aʊtbɔːd 'məʊtə(r)/ 43/13
outside /,aʊt'saɪd/ 47/20, 24; 76/1
,outside 'lane 39/5
oval /'əʊvl/ 68/F
oven /'ʌvn/ 30/2
over /'əʊvə(r)/ 77/7
overtake /,əʊvə'teɪk/ 66/13
owl /aʊl/ 60/7
oyster /'ɔɪstə(r)/ 58/16

Pacific /pə'sɪfɪk/ 6/9, 10
pack /pæk/ 52/10
packet /'pækɪt/ 73/10,11
pad /pæd/ 21/4, 23; 48/12
paddle /'pædl/ 43/9
page /peɪdʒ/ 52/19
paint /peɪnt/ 18/27; 65/4
'paintbrush 18/25
palette /'pælət/ 18/26
palm /pɑːm/ 8/28; 63/19
pan /pæn/ 19/2; 30/11, 12
pane /peɪn/ 26/10
panel /'pænl/ 45/28
pannier /'pænɪə(r)/ 40/34
†pants /pænts/ 10/2; 12/3
papaya /pə'paɪə/ 61/25
paper /'peɪpə(r)/ 21/10, 20; 22/12; 24/3; 33/9
,paper-'bag 67/7
'paper-clip 21/9
parachute /'pærəʃuːt/ 45/25
parallel /'pærəlel/ 68/5
parcel /'pɑːsl/ 22/20
park /pɑːk/ 14/12, 32
parking-meter /'pɑːkɪŋ miːtə(r)/ 15/25

parrot /'pærət/ 60/20
party /'pɑːtɪ/ 72/11
pass /pɑːs/ 66/13
passenger /'pæsɪndʒə(r)/ 41/19; 44/6
passport /'pɑːspɔːt/ 44/3
path /pɑːθ/ 27/18; 34/7
patient /'peɪʃnt/ 17/20
patio /'pætɪəʊ/ 26/5
pattern /'pætən/ 53/20
pavement /'peɪvmənt/ 15/29
paw /pɔː/ 56/17
pawn /pɔːn/ 52/3
pawpaw /'pɔːpɔː/ 61/25
pea /piː/ 62/3
peach /piːtʃ/ 61/19
peacock /'piːkɒk/ 60/11
peak /piːk/ 34/3
peanut /'piːnʌt/ 61/11
pear /peə(r)/ 61/22
pebble /'pebl/ 35/28
pedal /'pedl/ 40/17; 49/17
pedestrian crossing /pɪ'destrɪən 'krɒsɪŋ/ 14/2
‡peel /piːl/ 61/3, 18
peg /peg/ 27/30; 28/14
pelvis /'pelvɪs/ 8/7
pen /pen/ 18/17; 36/5
penalty /'penltɪ/ 47/10, 11
pencil /'pensl/ 18/15
penguin /'peŋgwɪn/ 60/13
penknife /'pennaɪf/ 24/5
pepper /'pepə(r)/ 51/29
per cent /pə 'sent/ 69/20
perfume /'pɜːfjuːm/ 12/16
periscope /'perɪskəʊp/ 45/20
perpendicular /ˌpɜːpən'dɪkjʊlə(r)/ 68/4
Persian Gulf /ˌpɜːʃn 'gʌlf/ 6/26
pestle /'pesl/ 19/20
petal /'petl/ 62/20
petrol-cap /'petrəl kæp/ 38/3
'petrol gauge 38/13
'petrol-pump 39/8
'petrol-station 39/7
petticoat /'petɪkəʊt/ 12/2
phase /feɪz/ 4/B
pheasant /'feznt/ 60/14
phone /fəʊn/ 28/25
'phone-box 15/31
phonetic /fə'netɪk/ 81
photo /'fəʊtəʊ/ 52/22
photograph /'fəʊtəgrɑːf/ 52/22
photographer /fə'tɒgrəfə(r)/ 55/4
‡photography /fə'tɒgrəfɪ/ 52/D
piano /pɪ'ænəʊ/ 49/15
pick /pɪk/ 66/8
'pick-axe 23/12
picture /'pɪktʃə(r)/ 29/12
piece /piːs/ 52/1; 73/8
pier /pɪə(r)/ 42/2
pig /pɪg/ 56/3
pigeon /'pɪdʒɪn/ 60/31
pile /paɪl/ 72/11
pill /pɪl/ 17/29
pillar-box /'pɪlə bɒks/ 22/4
pillow /'pɪləʊ/ 32/3
'pillow-case 32/4
'pillow-slip 32/4
pilot /'paɪlət/ 45/27
pin /pɪn/ 30/18; 53/10, 12
pincer /'pɪnsə(r)/ 58/18
†pincers /'pɪnsəz/ 24/14
pineapple /'paɪnæpl/ 61/24
pink /pɪŋk/ 79
pipe /paɪp/ 23/9; 26/17; 40/35
pipeline 37/12
pipette /pɪ'pet/ 19/18
pistol /'pɪstl/ 45/10
pit /pɪt/ 50/12
pitch /pɪtʃ/ 47/6; 48/13
plane /pleɪn/ 25/2; 44/9; 45/21
planet /'plænɪt/ 4/4
plank /plæŋk/ 23/11
plant /plɑːnt/ 61–63
plate /pleɪt/ 72/13
plateau /'plætəʊ/ 34/1
platform /'plætfɔːm/ 18/6; 41/20, 21
player /'pleɪə(r)/ 29/11; 46/24; 47/17, 18, 19; 49/3
playing-card /'pleɪɪŋ kɑːd/ 52/10
pleat /pliːt/ 53/11
†pliers /'plaɪəz/ 25/19
plimsoll /'plɪmsɒl/ 10/15
plough /plaʊ/ 36/19
plug /plʌg/ 31/15; 33/6; 38/35

plug-hole /'plʌg həʊl/ 33/5
plum /plʌm/ 61/23
plus /plʌs/ 69/15
pneumatic drill /njuːˌmætɪk 'drɪl/ 23/23
pocket /'pɒkɪt/ 11/16
pod /pɒd/ 62/4; 63/4
point /pɔɪnt/ 69/21
pointer /'pɔɪntə(r)/ 19/6
†points /pɔɪnts/ 41/26
pole /pəʊl/ 43/11; 47/27
Pole /pəʊl/ 5/1, 7
police /pə'liːs/ 16
po'lice-car 16/5
po'lice-dog 16/6
po'liceman 16/1; 55/13
po'lice-station 16/4
pond /pɒnd/ 34/19; 36/9
pop group /'pɒp gruːp/ 49/B
porter /'pɔːtə(r)/ 54/14
possessive /pə'zesɪv/ 78
postal order /'pəʊstl ɔːdə(r)/ 22/17
post-box /'pəʊst bɒks/ 22/4
postcard /'pəʊstkɑːd/ 22/13
poster /'pəʊstə(r)/ 18/24
postman /'pəʊstmən/ 22/5
postmark /'pəʊstmɑːk/ 22/8
post office /'pəʊst ɒfɪs/ 22
pot /pɒt/ 29/33; 30/12; 51/28, 29
potato /pə'teɪtəʊ/ 62/6
potty /'pɒtɪ/ 32/32
pouch /paʊtʃ/ 57/7
powder /'paʊdə(r)/ 31/9, 18
'powder-compact 12/13
‡power /'paʊə(r)/ 37
'power-house 37/3
'power-point 31/16
'power station 37/6
pram /præm/ 14/18
preposition /prepə'zɪʃn/ 76–77
press-stud /'pres stʌd/ 53/27
pretty /'prɪtɪ/ 75/9
print /prɪnt/ 52/22
prison /'prɪzn/ 16/B
prisoner /'prɪznə(r)/ 16/14
profession /prə'feʃn/ 54–55
projectionist /prə'dʒekʃənɪst/ 50/16
projection room /prə'dʒekʃn rʊm/ 50/14
projector /prə'dʒektə(r)/ 50/15; 52/29
promenade /ˌprɒmə'nɑːd/ 35/9
pronoun /'prəʊnaʊn/ 78
pronunciation /prəˌnʌnsɪ'eɪʃn/ 81
propeller /prə'pelə(r)/ 43/14; 44/18
protractor /prə'træktə(r)/ 18/12
pull /pʊl/ 65/5
pullover /'pʊləʊvə(r)/ 13/5
pump /pʌmp/ 40/16; 51/19
punch /pʌntʃ/ 21/6
punt /pʌnt/ 43/10
pupil /'pjuːpl/ 9/19; 18/8
puppy /'pʌpɪ/ 56/14
purple /'pɜːpl/ 79
purse /pɜːs/ 67/6
push /pʊʃ/ 65/6
put /pʊt/ 66/15
†pyjamas /pə'dʒɑːməz/ 10/4
pylon /'paɪlən/ 37/5
pyramid /'pɪrəmɪd/ 68/22

quantity /'kwɒntɪtɪ/ 72–73
quarter /'kwɔːtə(r)/ 69/14; 70/7, 9
quay /kiː/ 42/5
queen /kwiːn/ 52/7, 12

rabbit /'ræbɪt/ 56/20
race-horse /'reɪs hɔːs/ 46/2
rack /ræk/ 28/13; 30/10; 41/9
racket /'rækɪt/ 48/21
radiator /'reɪdɪeɪtə(r)/ 38/33
'radiator grill 38/27
radio /'reɪdɪəʊ/ 29/22; 38/25
radius /'reɪdɪəs/ 68/17
rafter /'rɑːftə(r)/ 23/3
rail /reɪl/ 33/21
railway-line /'reɪlweɪ laɪn/ 41/24
‡train /reɪn/ 27/3
'raincoat 11/12
'raindrop 27/4
rat /ræt/ 56/22
rattle /'rætl/ 32/30
razor /'reɪzə(r)/ 33/12
'razor-blade 33/13
read /riːd/ 65/7
reading /'riːdɪŋ/ 52/C

rear /rɪə(r)/ 38/1; 40/30
receipt /rɪ'siːt/ 20/23
receiver /rɪ'siːvə(r)/ 28/26
record /'rekɔːd/ 29/20
'record-player 29/11
‡recreation /ˌrekrɪ'eɪʃn/ 46–52
rectangle /'rektæŋgl/ 68/D
red /red/ 79
Red Sea /ˌred 'siː/ 6/25
reel /riːl/ 53/8; 73/9
referee /ˌrefə'riː/ 46/10; 47/3
refinery /rɪ'faɪnərɪ/ 37/13
reflector /rɪ'flektə(r)/ 40/20
refrigerator /rɪ'frɪdʒəreɪtə(r)/ 30/5
reindeer /'reɪndɪə(r)/ 56/11
†reins /reɪnz/ 40/24; 46/4
relationship /rɪ'leɪʃnʃɪp/ 71
reptile /'reptaɪl/ 59/A
reservoir /'rezəvwɑː(r)/ 37/1
restaurant /'restərɒnt/ 51
revolver /rɪ'vɒlvə(r)/ 45/12
rhinoceros /raɪ'nɒsərəs/ 57/25
rib /rɪb/ 8/5
ribbon /'rɪbn/ 53/24
‡rice /raɪs/ 63/7
ride /raɪd/ 65/8
rifle /'raɪfl/ 45/2
rig /rɪg/ 37/11
right /raɪt/ 47/16, 19, 23, 24
'right angle 68/14
rind /raɪnd/ 61/18
ring /rɪŋ/ 12/18; 30/4; 46/13
river /'rɪvə(r)/ 7/F; 34/12
road /rəʊd/ 15/34; 34/18
robe /rəʊb/ 16/24
rock /rɒk/ 35/29
rocket /'rɒkɪt/ 4/16
Rockies /'rɒkɪz/ 7/36
rod /rɒd/ 48/19
roll /rəʊl/ 52/24; 73/12
rolling-pin /'rəʊlɪŋ pɪn/ 30/18
roof /ruːf/ 26/1
rook /rʊk/ 52/4
room /rʊm/ 29; 32; 33; 41/18
root /ruːt/ 63/11
rope /rəʊp/ 46/14
rose /rəʊz/ 62/19
rostrum /'rɒstrəm/ 49/13
rotor /'rəʊtə(r)/ 44/16
rough /rʌf/ 75/4, 5
round /raʊnd/ 76/6
'roundabout 39/4
row /rəʊ/ 72/14
rowing-boat /'rəʊɪŋ bəʊt/ 43/6
rubber /'rʌbə(r)/ 18/14
rubbish-bin /'rʌbɪʃ bɪn/ 30/9
rucksack /'rʌksæk/ 35/4
Rugby /'rʌgbɪ/ 46/H
rug /rʌg/ 28/12; 32/16
ruler /'ruːlə(r)/ 18/10
run /rʌn/ 65/9
rung /rʌŋ/ 23/6
runway /'rʌnweɪ/ 44/19

sack /sæk/ 67/13
sad /sæd/ 74/11
saddle /'sædl/ 40/7; 46/3
'saddlebag 40/8
safe /seɪf/ 67/20
safety-belt /'seɪftɪ belt/ 38/24
'safety-pin 53/10
Sahara /sə'hɑːrə/ 7/41
sail /seɪl/ 43/4; 65/10
sailor /'seɪlə(r)/ 55/15
salesman /'seɪlzmən/ 55/9
‡†salmon /'sæmən/ 58/4
saloon /sə'luːn/ 38/37
salt /sɔːlt/ 51/27
‡sand /sænd/ 23/15; 35/22
sandal /'sændl/ 13/7
'sandpaper 24/3
satchel /'sætʃl/ 18/9
satellite /'sætəlaɪt/ 4/18
Saturday /'sætədɪ/ 80
saucepan /'sɔːspən/ 30/12
saucer /'sɔːsə(r)/ 29/31
sausage /'sɒsɪdʒ/ 20/12
saw /sɔː/ 25/17
saxophone /'sæksəfəʊn/ 49/22
‡scaffolding /'skæfəldɪŋ/ 23/7
scale /skeɪl/ 58/9
scales /skeɪlz/ 19/1; 22/2; 30/17; 33/22

scarecrow /'skeəkrəʊ/ 36/13
scarf /skɑːf/ 11/19; 13/13
‡scent /sent/ 12/16
school /skuːl/ 18
'schoolbag 18/9
'schoolgirl 18/8
science /'saɪəns/ 19
†scissors /'sɪzəz/ 53/26
scooter /'skuːtə(r)/ 40/29
scorpion /'skɔːpɪən/ 58/27
scourer /'skaʊrə(r)/ 30/26
‡scouring powder /'skaʊrɪŋ paʊdə(r)/ 31/9
screen /skriːn/ 29/18; 50/18; 52/27
screw /skruː/ 25/9
screwdriver /'skruːdraɪvə(r)/ 24/7
scrubbing-brush /'skrʌbɪŋ brʌʃ/ 31/10
sea /siː/ 6–7/C; 35/31
'sea-front 35/9
'seagull 60/21
seal /siːl/ 22/18; 57/9
‡sealing-wax /'siːlɪŋ wæks/ 22/19
seam /siːm/ 53/3
‡seaside 35/B
seat /siːt/ 38/23; 40/31; 41/8; 50/20
'seat-belt 38/24
,sea-'wall 35/10
‡seaweed /'siːwiːd/ 35/37
second /'sekənd/ 70/3; 80
secretary /'sekrətrɪ/ 21/22
sector /'sektə(r)/ 68/21
seed /siːd/ 62/28
segment /'segmənt/ 61/17
September /sep'tembə(r)/ 80
server /'sɜːvə(r)/ 48/25
service /'sɜːvɪs/ 17; 48/26
'service-station 39/7
serviette /ˌsɜːvɪ'et/ 51/31
set /set/ 50/4
'set-square 18/16
settee /se'tiː/ 29/21
seven /'sevn/ 80
seventeen /ˌsevn'tiːn/ 80
seventh /'sevnθ/ 80
seventy /'sevntɪ/ 80
sew /səʊ/ 65/11
sewing /'səʊɪŋ/ 53
'sewing-machine 53/1
shallow /'ʃæləʊ/ 74/6
shape /ʃeɪp/ 68
shark /ʃɑːk/ 58/1
sharp /ʃɑːp/ 74/2
shaving-brush /'ʃeɪvɪŋ brʌʃ/ 33/14
shawl /ʃɔːl/ 12/5
she /ʃiː/ 79
†shears /ʃɪəz/ 24/11
shed /ʃed/ 26/20; 27/26
‡†sheep /ʃiːp/ 36/29
'sheepdog 36/28
sheet /ʃiːt/ 21/10; 32/5; 49/12
shelf /ʃelf/ 20/15; 30/16
shell /ʃel/ 35/27; 45/7; 58/14; 59/5
shepherd /'ʃepəd/ 36/26
ship /ʃɪp/ 42/7
shirt /ʃɜːt/ 11/1
shoe /ʃuː/ 10/9; 11/8; 13/12
shoelace /'ʃuːleɪs/ 11/9
shoot /ʃuːt/ 65/12
shop /ʃɒp/ 15/22
'shop-assistant 20/8
'shopping basket 67/10
,shop-'window 15/23; 20/1
short /ʃɔːt/ 74/16
†shorts /ʃɔːts/ 10/12
shoulder /'ʃəʊldə(r)/ 8/13
'shoulder-blade 8/3
shovel /'ʃʌvl/ 23/13
shower /'ʃaʊə(r)/ 33/4
shrub /ʃrʌb/ 27/22
shut /ʃʌt/ 65/13; 74/4
shutter /'ʃʌtə(r)/ 26/12
side /saɪd/ 68/13; 69/5
siding /'saɪdɪŋ/ 41/30
sieve /sɪv/ 30/30
signal /'sɪgnl/ 41/27
'signal-box 41/23
'signalman 41/22
signpost /'saɪnpəʊst/ 14/8
sill /sɪl/ 26/11
sing /sɪŋ/ 65/14
singer /'sɪŋə(r)/ 49/24
sink /sɪŋk/ 30/7
sister /'sɪstə(r)/ 71/5
sister-in-law /'sɪstər ɪn lɔː/ 71/8

sit /sɪt/ 65/15
site /saɪt/ 23
sitting-room /'sɪtɪŋ rʊm/ 29
six /sɪks/ 80
sixteen /ˌsɪks'tiːn/ 80
sixth /sɪksθ/ 80
sixty /'sɪkstɪ/ 80
skate /skeɪt/ 47/31
skater /'skeɪtə(r)/ 47/30
skeleton /'skelɪtn/ 8/A
ski /skiː/ 47/26
skier /'skiːə(r)/ 47/25
‡skin /skɪn/ 61/6
skip /skɪp/ 23/24
'ski-pole 47/27
skirt /skɜːt/ 13/2
'ski-stick 47/27
skull /skʌl/ 8/1
sky /skaɪ/ 27/10
sleep /sliːp/ 66/19
sleeper /'sliːpə(r)/ 41/25
sleeping-bag /'sliːpɪŋ bæg/ 35/3
'sleeping suit 32/27
sleeve /sliːv/ 11/7
slice /slaɪs/ 73/8
slide /slaɪd/ 19/11; 49/21; 52/30
'slide-projector 52/29
'slide-rule 18/20
sling /slɪŋ/ 17/23
slip /slɪp/ 12/2; 32/4
slipper /'slɪpə(r)/ 10/5; 12/7
slow /sləʊ/ 74/9
slug /slʌg/ 58/19
small /smɔːl/ 74/1
smile /smaɪl/ 65/16
‡smoke /sməʊk/ 17/12
smooth /smuːð/ 75/5
snail /sneɪl/ 58/13
snake /sneɪk/ 59/6
snapshot /'snæpʃɒt/ 52/22
snorkel /'snɔːkl/ 35/16
snout /snaʊt/ 56/4
‡snow /snəʊ/ 27/5
'snowball 27/6
'snowman 27/7
‡soap /səʊp/ 33/25
‡soap powder /'səʊp paʊdə(r)/ 31/18
‡soccer /'sɒkə(r)/ 47/A
sock /sɒk/ 10/14; 13/3
socket /'sɒkɪt/ 31/16
sofa /'səʊfə/ 29/21
soft /sɒft/ 51/13; 74/13
soldier /'səʊldʒə(r)/ 45/1; 55/12
sole /səʊl/ 9/40; 11/10
solid /'sɒlɪd/ 68/G; 75/14
son /sʌn/ 71/3
son-in-law /'sʌn ɪn lɔː/ 71/7
south /saʊθ/ 5/C
,South ,China 'Sea 7/31
southeast /ˌsaʊθ'iːst/ 5/C
Southern /'sʌðən/ 6/14
,South 'Pole 5/7
southwest /ˌsaʊθ'west/ 5/C
‡space /speɪs/ 4/A
'space-capsule 4/19
'spacesuit 4/21
‡'space-travel 4/C
spade /speɪd/ 24/9; 35/25; 52/14
spanner /'spænə(r)/ 24/13
sparking-plug /'spɑːkɪŋ plʌg/ 38/35
sparrow /'spærəʊ/ 60/22
speedometer /spɪ'dɒmɪtə(r)/ 38/16
spider /'spaɪdə(r)/ 58/25
spin /spɪn/ 66/16
spine /spaɪn/ 8/6; 52/18
spiral /'spaɪərəl/ 68/1
spoke /spəʊk/ 40/12
sponge /spʌndʒ/ 33/24
spoon /spuːn/ 17/31; 29/27
sport /spɔːt/ 46–48
sportscar /'spɔːtskɑː(r)/ 39/18
spot /spɒt/ 47/11
'spotlight 50/7
spout /spaʊt/ 29/34
square /skweə(r)/ 68/C
squirrel /'skwɪrəl/ 56/19
stadium /'steɪdɪəm/ 47/B
stage /steɪdʒ/ 50/1
stair /steə(r)/ 28/16
'staircase 28/17
stalk /stɔːk/ 61/2; 62/2
stall /stɔːl/ 14/3
stalls /stɔːlz/ 50/11

stamp /stæmp/ 22/9
stand /stænd/ 47/5; 52/28; 65/17
staple /'steɪpl/ 21/8
stapler /'steɪplə(r)/ 21/7
star /stɑː(r)/ 4/5
starter /'stɑːtə(r)/ 40/36
station /'steɪʃn/ 41/13
steering-wheel /'stɪərɪŋ wiːl/ 38/17
stem /stem/ 62/23
stethoscope /'steθəskəʊp/ 17/22
stick /stɪk/ 46/18; 47/27
stir /stɜː(r)/ 65/18
stirrup /'stɪrəp/ 46/7
stitch /stɪtʃ/ 53/17
stomach /'stʌmək/ 8/17
stone /stəʊn/ 61/8, 20
stool /stuːl/ 19/8; 32/11; 49/18; 51/20
storage tank /'stɔːrɪdʒ tæŋk/ 37/14
storm-cloud /'stɔːm klaʊd/ 27/2
stove /stəʊv/ 30/1; 35/5
straight /streɪt/ 68/2; 74/5
strainer /'streɪnə(r)/ 30/30
straw /strɔː/ 51/12
strawberry /'strɔːbrɪ/ 61/21
stream /striːm/ 34/7
street /striːt/ 15/34
stress /stres/ 81
stretcher /'stretʃə(r)/ 17/32
striker /'straɪkə(r)/ 47/20–24
‡string /strɪŋ/ 22/21; 49/5; 72/8
strong /strɒŋ/ 75/6
stumps /stʌmps/ 48/9
submarine /ˌsʌbmə'riːn/ 45/19
sugar-bowl /'ʃʊgə bəʊl/ 29/39
‡sugar-cane /'ʃʊgə keɪn/ 63/9
suit /suːt/ 11/6; 46/23
'suitcase 67/17
sun /sʌn/ 4/8; 27/9
'sunbather 35/13
Sunday /'sʌndɪ/ 80
‡†'sunfish 58/15
'sunflower 62/27
'sunshade 35/12
supermarket /'suːpəmɑːkɪt/ 20
‡surf sɜːf/ 35/32
swallow /'swɒləʊ/ 60/22
swan /swɒn/ 60/17
swarm /swɔːm/ 72/16
sweater /'swetə(r)/ 13/5
sweep /swiːp/ 65/19
swim /swɪm/ 65/20
swimming /'swɪmɪŋ/
'swimming-costume 35/36
'swimming trunks 35/20
switch /swɪtʃ/ 28/23; 31/17
'switchboard 21/15
‡†swordfish /'sɔːdfɪʃ/ 58/3
symbol /'sɪmbl/ 81

T-shirt /'tiː ʃɜːt/ 10/11
table /'teɪbl/ 29/19, 23; 32/9, 10; 46/21
'table-cloth 51/30
'table-mat 29/25
tablet /'tæblɪt/ 73/3
‡'table-tennis 46/E
tail /teɪl/ 44/13; 56/23; 58/7
tank /tæŋk/ 37/14; 45/8; 67/21
tankard /'tæŋkəd/ 51/14
tanker /'tæŋkə(r)/ 39/19; 43/18
tap /tæp/ 33/2, 3
tape /teɪp/ 53/2
tape-measure 53/25
Tasman Sea /ˌtæzmən 'siː/ 6/30
taxi /'tæksɪ/ 14/5
tea /tiː/ 63/8
teacher /'tiːtʃə(r)/ 18/1; 55/11
team /tiːm/ 72/15
teapot 29/36
tear /teə(r)/ 65/21
teat /tiːt/ 32/34
'tea-towel 30/32
teddy-bear /'tedɪ beə(r)/ 32/29
telegram /'telɪgræm/ 22/16
telephone /'telɪfəʊn/ 21/2; 28/25
'telephone-box 15/31
'telephone directory 28/29
television /'telɪvɪʒn/ 29/17, 18
temperature /'temprətʃə(r)/ 70/C
temple /'templ/ 9/7
ten /ten/ 80
tennis /'tenɪs/ 46/E; 48/D
'tennis-ball 48/28
'tennis-shoe 10/15

tent /tent/ 35/1
tentacle /'tentəkl/ 58/24
tenth /tenθ/ 80
test-tube /'test tjuːb/ 19/22
text /tekst/ 52/21
'textbook 18/19
that /ðæt/ 79
theatre /'θɪətə(r)/ 50/8
their /ðeə(r)/ 79
theirs /ðeəz/ 79
them /ðəm, ðem/ 79
there /ðeə(r)/ 79
thermometer /θə'mɒmɪtə(r)/ 17/28; 70/12
thermos flask /'θɜːməs flɑːsk/ 67/9
these ði:z/ 79
they /ðeɪ/ 79
thick /θɪk/ 75/15
thigh /θaɪ/ 8/33
thimble /'θɪmbl/ 53/5
thin /θɪn/ 74/10; 75/15
third /θɜːd/ 69/13; 80
thirteen /ˌθɜː'tiːn/ 80
thirty /'θɜːtɪ/ 80
this /ðɪs/ 79
those /ðəʊz/ 79
thousand /'θaʊznd/ 80
thread /θred/ 25/10
three /θriː/ 80
throat θrəʊt/ 8/12
throttle /'θrɒtl/ 40/32
through /θruː/ 76/2
throw /θrəʊ/ 66/9
thumb /θʌm/ 8/29
thunder-cloud /'θʌndə klaʊd/ 27/2
Thursday /'θɜːzdɪ/ 80
ticket /'tɪkɪt/ 41/7
'ticket-collector 41/16
'ticket-inspector 41/16
'ticket-office 41/14
tidy /'taɪdɪ/ 75/7
tie /taɪ/ 11/4; 65/23
tiger /'taɪgə(r)/ 57/19
tight /taɪt/ 75/16
†tights /taɪts/ 12/4
tile /taɪl/ 23/4
time /taɪm/ 70/A; 80
'timetable 18/22; 41/15
tin /tɪn/ 30/19, 22
tinned food /ˌtɪnd 'fuːd/ 20/16
'tin-opener 30/21
tipper-truck /'tɪpə trʌk/ 23/22
tissue /'tɪʃuː/ 32/22
to /tə, tuː/ 77/4
toboggan /tə'bɒgən/ 47/29
tobogganist /tə'bɒgənɪst/ 47/28
toe /təʊ/ 9/41
toilet /'tɔɪlɪt/ 33/7
‡'toilet-paper 33/9
'toilet-roll 33/9
tomato /tə'mɑːtəʊ/ 62/15
tongue /tʌŋ/ 9/14; 59/8
tool /tuːl/ 25
tooth /tuːθ/ 9/12
'toothbrush 33/15
'toothmug 33/16
‡'toothpaste 33/19
top /tɒp/ 51/2; 69/1
torch /tɔːtʃ/ 16/9
torpedo /tɔː'piːdəʊ/ 45/17
tortoise /'tɔːtəs/ 59/2
touch /tʌtʃ/ 65/22
'touch-line 47/12
towards /tə'wɔːdz/ 77/10
towel /'taʊəl/ 33/20; 35/14
'towel-rail 33/21
town /taʊn/ 14-15
tractor /'træktə(r)/ 36/18
traffic-light /'træfɪk laɪt/ 14/7
trailer /'treɪlə(r)/ 39/21
train /treɪn/ 41
transporter /træn'spɔːtə(r)/ 39/12
travel /'trævl/ 38-44
trawler /'trɔːlə(r)/ 43/17
tray /treɪ/ 30/14
tree /triː/ 27/11; 34/15; 63/10
triangle /'traɪæŋgl/ 68/B
trigger /'trɪgə(r)/ 45/13
tripod /'traɪpɒd/ 19/13
trombone /trɒm'bəʊn/ 49/20
Tropic /'trɒpɪk/ 5/3, 5
†trousers /'traʊzəz/ 11/17; 13/6
trowel /'traʊəl/ 23/17; 24/12
truck /trʌk/ 23/22; 41/28
trumpet /'trʌmpɪt/ 49/19

truncheon /'trʌntʃən/ 16/7
trunk /trʌŋk/ 27/12; 57/22; 63/12; 67/12
†trunks /trʌŋks/ 35/20
T-shirt /'tiː ʃɜːt/ 10/11
tube /tjuːb/ 19/22; 33/19; 73/13
tubing /'tjuːbɪŋ/ 19/14
Tuesday /'tjuːzdɪ/ 80
tug /tʌg/ 42/19
tulip /'tjuːlɪp/ 62/22
tummy /'tʌmɪ/ 8/17
turkey /'tɜːkɪ/ 60/16
turn /tɜːn/ 66/10
'turn-up 11/18
turtle /'tɜːtl/ 59/4
tusk /tʌsk/ 57/23
‡TV /ˌtiː 'viː/ 29/17
twelve /twelv/ 80
twentieth /'twentɪəθ/ 80
twenty /'twentɪ/ 80
,twenty-'one 80
twig /twɪg/ 27/14; 63/14
two /tuː/ 80
type /taɪp/ 66/21
typewriter /'taɪpraɪtə(r)/ 21/21
typist /'taɪpɪst/ 21/22; 54/9
tyre /'taɪə(r)/ 38/8; 40/11

ugly /'ʌglɪ/ 75/9
umbrella /ʌm'brelə/ 11/24; 13/17
umpire /'ʌmpaɪə(r)/ 48/16
uncle /'ʌŋkl/ 71/10
under /'ʌndə(r)/ 76/17
,under'neath 76/17
'underpass 39/3
uniform /'juːnɪfɔːm/ 16/3
universe /'juːnɪvɜːs/ 4
untidy /ʌn'taɪdɪ/ 75/7
up /ʌp/ 76/5
,up'stairs 28/20
Urals /'jʊərəlz/ 7/39
urn /ɜːn/ 67/2
us /əs, ʌs/ 79
usherette /ˌʌʃə'ret/ 50/19

vacuum-flask /'vækjʊəm flɑːsk/ 67/9
vacuum-cleaner /'vækjʊəm kliːnə(r)/ 31/1
valley /'vælɪ/ 34/6
valve /vælv/ 40/13
van /væn/ 14/14; 39/22
vase /vɑːz/ 29/14
vegetable /'vedʒtəbl/ 20/18; 62
'vegetable-rack 30/10
vein /veɪn/ 9/29
verb /vɜːb/ 64-66
vest /vest/ 10/1
vice /vaɪs/ 24/8
village /'vɪlɪdʒ/ 34/16
vine /vaɪn/ 61/13
viola /vɪ'əʊlə/ 49/7
violin /ˌvaɪə'lɪn/ 49/4
vowel /'vaʊəl/ 82
vulture /'vʌltʃə(r)/ 60/10

waggon /'wægən/ 41/28
waist /weɪst/ 8/16
waistcoat /'weɪskəʊt/ 11/5
waiter /'weɪtə(r)/ 51/21
waiting-room /'weɪtɪŋ rʊm/ 41/18
waitress /'weɪtrəs/ 54/11
walk /wɔːk/ 65/24
wall /wɔːl/ 26/3; 29/2
wallet /'wɒlɪt/ 67/16
walnut /'wɔːlnʌt/ 61/27
ward /wɔːd/ 17/C
warder /'wɔːdə(r)/ 16/13
wardrobe /'wɔːdrəʊb/ 32/14
warehouse /'weəhaʊs/ 42/3
warship /'wɔːʃɪp/ 45/16
wash /wɒʃ/ 65/25
'wash-basin 33/11
washer /'wɒʃə(r)/ 25/12
‡washing /'wɒʃɪŋ/ 27/29
'washing-line 27/28
'washing-machine 31/4
,washing-'up brush 30/27
‡,washing-'up liquid 30/28
wasp /wɒsp/ 57/24
wastepaper basket /ˌweɪst 'peɪpə bɑːskɪt/ 21/13
'waste-pipe 23/9
watch /wɒtʃ/ 11/21
'watch-strap 11/22
water /'wɔːtə(r)/ 42-43
'waterfall 34/4

watering-can /'wɔːtərɪŋ kæn/ 27/23
'waterlily 62/26
wave /weɪv/ 35/33; 66/1
wavy /'weɪvɪ/ 68/7
wax /wæks/ 22/19
we /wiː/ 79
weak /wiːk/ 75/6
‡weather /'weðə(r)/ 27
web /web/ 58/26
webbed /webd/ 60/9
Wednesday /'wenzdɪ/ 80
week /wiːk/ 80
weep /wiːp/ 64/7
weight /weɪt/ 19/3; 80
wellington /'welɪŋtən/ 10/10
west /west/ 5/C
wet /wet/ 74/7
whale /weɪl/ 57/1
wharf /wɔːf/ 42/5
what /wɒt/ 79
‡wheat /wiːt/ 36/14; 63/2
wheel /wiːl/ 40/9
'wheelbarrow 27/27
where /weə(r)/ 79
which /wɪtʃ/ 79
whip /wɪp/ 40/25
whisker /'wɪskə(r)/ 56/21
whistle /'wɪsl/ 41/12; 47/4
white /waɪt/ 79
who /huː/ 79
whose /huːz/ 79
wicket /'wɪkɪt/ 48/9, 11
wide /waɪd/ 75/1
width /wɪdθ/ 69/8
wife /waɪf/ 71/1
wig /wɪg/ 16/25
willow /'wɪləʊ/ 63/24
wind /waɪnd/ 66/3
windbreak 35/18
windlass /'wɪndləs/ 42/16
window /'wɪndəʊ/ 15/23; 26/8
'window-box 26/13
'window-frame 26/9
'window-ledge 26/11
'window-pane 26/10
'window-sill 26/11
'windpipe 9/22
windscreen 38/10
'windscreen-wiper 38/11
wine /waɪn/ 51/24
wing /wɪŋ/ 44/11; 60/23
wings /wɪŋz/ 50/5
†winter sports /ˌwɪntə 'spɔːts/ 47/D
witness /'wɪtnɪs/ 16/19
'witness-box 16/18
wolf /wʊlf/ 57/11
woman /'wʊmən/ 12-13
wood /wʊd/ 34/8
‡wool /wʊl/ 53/19
workbench /'wɜːkbentʃ/ 24/1
workman /'wɜːkmən/ 23/14
workshop /'wɜːkʃɒp/ 24
world /wɜːld/ 5-7
worm /wɜːm/ 58/21
wrench /rentʃ/ 24/6
wrestler /'reslə(r)/ 46/22
‡wrestling /'reslɪŋ/ 46/F
wrist /rɪst/ 8/25
write /raɪt/ 66/2
‡writing-paper /'raɪtɪŋ peɪpə(r)/ 22/12

x-ray /ˌeks 'reɪ/ 17/24

yacht /jɒt/ 43/1
Yangtze /'jæŋtsɪ/ 7/55
year /jɜː(r)/ 80
yellow /'jeləʊ/ 79
Yellow River /ˌjeləʊ 'rɪvə(r)/ 7/54
you /jə, juː/ 79
young /jʌŋ/ 75/2
your /jɔː(r)/ 79
yours /jɔːz/ 79

zebra /'ziːbrə/ 57/24
zero /'zɪərəʊ/ 80
zig-zag /'zɪg zæg/ 68/6
zip /zɪp/ 53/22
'zip-fastener 53/22
zipper /'zɪpə(r)/ 53/22

A
a través 76/2
abajo 69/2; 76/4
abalorios 72/8
abeja 59/21
abeto 63/20
abierto 74/4
abogado 16/23
abrazar 66/6
abrebotellas 51/7
abrelatas 30/21
abrigo 11/14; 13/9
abril 80
abrir 65/2
acantilado 35/6
acelerador 38/18; 40/32
acera 15/29
acomodadora 50/19
actor 50/2
actriz 50/3
adjetivo 74
aduana 44/1
aduanero 44/2
adverbio 79
aerodeslizador 42/18
aeroplano 44/9
afilado 74/2
África 6/4
agalla 58/5
agarrar 64/4
agitado 75/4
agitar 65/4
agosto 80
agua 42–43
aguja 5/16; 19/6; 41/26; 55/6;
  53/18; 63/22
aguila 60/2
ahogarse 64/16
ajedrez 52/A
al 77/4
ala 44/11; 60/23
Alaska 6/15
albañil 23/2
alcantarilla 14/11
aldaba 28/2
alejado 77/11
aleta 57/2, 4, 10; 58/2
alféizar 26/11
alfil 52/6
alfiler 53/12
alfombra 29/3; 32/16
alfombrilla 28/12
alga 35/37
algodón 63/6
alicates 25/19
alimentos 20/16
alineación 47/C
almacén 42/3
almohada 32/3
almohadón 32/4
Alpes 7/38
alrededor 76/6
altavoz 49/28
alto 74/14
altura 69/9
alumna 18/8
amarillo 7/54; 79
Amazonas 7/16
ambulancia 39/15
América 6/12, 13
ametralladora 45/15
amplificador 49/27
amplio 74/1
ananás 61/24
ancla 42/11
ancho 75/1
anchura 69/8
andamio 23/7
andén 41/20
Andes 7/37
anfiteatro 50/10
anguila 58/10
ángulo 68
animal 56
antártico 5/6
Antártida 6/7
antebrazo 8/24
antena 26/19; 38/9; 59/16, 22
anteojeras 40/27
anteojos 33/45
antílope 57/5
anunciador 54/15
anuncio 15/21

anzuelo 48/21
año 81
aparcadero 41/30
aplaudir 66/17
apretado 75/16
Arabia 6/27; 7/43
arado 36/19
arandela 25/12
araña 58/25
árbitro 46/10; 47/3
árbol 27/11; 34/15; 36/11
arbusto 27/22
archivador 21/19
arco 49/6; 68/16
ardilla 56/19
arena 23/15; 35/22
arenque 58/6
armario 32/14
armarito 32/13
arranque 40/36
arrastrar 64/6
arreos 40/23
arriba 69/1
arrodillarse 64/23
arrojar 66/9
arroz 63/7
artesa 23/18
ártico 5/2; 6/8
artista 54/8
as 52/14
asa 29/38
Asia 6/5
asiento 38/23; 40/31; 41/8;
  50/20
áspero 75/5
aspirador 31/1
asta 56/12
astronauta 4/20
atar 65/23
Atlántico 6/11, 12
atracadero 48/12
auricular 28/26
Australia 6/6
autobus 15/26
autocar 39/17
automóvil 38; 38/37; 39/18
autopista 39/1
avestruz 60/1
avión 44/9; 44/17
avispa 59/22
ayudante 17/14
áxila 8/20
azadón 23/19
azafata 44/7
azúcar 63/9
azucarera 29/39
azul 79

B
babero 32/35
babosa 58/19
babuino 57/13
bahía 5/8; 6/C
bailar 66/17
bajo 74/14; 76/17
bala 45/11
balanza 19/1; 22/2; 30/17
balcón 26/4
balón 47/1
baloncesto 46/C
Báltico 6/21
ballena 57/1
banco 19/7; 24/1
bandada 72/6
bandeja 30/14
banquillo 16/18, 21
baño 33/1
bar 51/16
baraja 52/10
barandilla 28/18
barba 9/11; 56/21
barbero 55/6
barbilla 9/6
barca 43/10
barcaza 43/16
barco 42/7
barman 51/18
barra 16/16; 40/15; 73/2, 3
barrena 25/6
barrer 65/19
barril 67/4
báscula 33/22

base 68/9
baseball 48/A
bastidor 50/5
basto 52/11
bastón 46/18; 47/27
basura 30/9
batería 38/32
batín 10/3
batuta 49/11
baúl 67/12
bayoneta 45/3
bebé 32/B
beber 64/13
bebida 51/13
bellota 63/16
Bengala 6/28
berbequí 25/5
berenjena 62/16
Bering 7/35
berza 62/11
besar 66/7
biberón 32/33
biblioteca 50/C
bibliotecario 50/23
bicicleta 14/6; 40/1
bigote 9/10; 56/21
billete 20/24; 41/7
bisagra 28/9
blanco 79
blando 74/13
bloc de notas 21/23
bloque 15/19, 20
blusa 13/1
boca 9/4; 17/5
bocado 46/6
bodega 42/8
bola 27/6; 48/28
bolsa 20/6; 40/8; 57/7; 67/7, 15
bolsillo 11/16
bolso 13/16; 67/5
bomba 39/9; 40/16; 45/24;
  51/19
bombardero 45/23
bombero 17/1
bombilla 31/13
bonito 75/9
boquilla 49/23
borde 69/4
bordillo 14/9
borrador 18/5
bosque 34/8, 9
bota 10/10
botella 51/1; 51/24
botón 53/15
boxeador 46/11
boxeo 46/B
boya 42/13
braga 12/3
branquia 58/5
brazo 8/21
brida 46/5
brocha 33/14
broche 13/15
brújula 5/C
bueno 75/8
búfalo 56/8
bufanda 11/19
buho 60/7
buitre 60/10
bujía 38/35
buque 43/18; 45/16
burro 56/10
butaca 29/8; 50/11
buzón 14/1; 22/4, 28/5

C
cabalgar 65/8
caballete 18/3
caballo 40/21; 46/2; 52/5; 56/1
cabecera 31/2
cabello 8/9
cabestrillo 17/23
cabeza 8/10; 25/15
cabina 15/31; 43/2
cable 31/12; 37/4; 40/4; 42/15
cabra 36/24
cacahuete 61/11
cacerola 30/12
cachorro 56/14
cactus 61/31
cadena 40/18
cadera 8/7, 18

caer 64/18
caja 17/29; 20/3, 4; 21/12;
  30/15; 51/5; 67; 73/10
cajera 20/2
cajetilla 73/10
calabacín 62/7
calcetín 13/3
calculadora 21/3
caldero 30/13
calendario 18/23; 21/17; 70/B
caliente 74/15
calle 15/34
cama 17/19; 32/1
camaleón 59/3
camarera 54/11
camarero 44/18; 51/21
camilla 17/32
caminar 65/25
camello 56/6
camión 14/15; 39
camioneta 14/14; 39/22
camisa 11/1
camiseta 10/1, 11
camisón 12/6
campana 17/9
camping 35/A
campo 34; 47/6
canal 36/17
canalón 26/16
canapé 29/21
canario 60/18
cáncer 5/3
candileja 50/13
cangrejo 58/17
canguro 57/6
canoa 43/8
cantante 49/24
cantar 65/14
cantidad 72
caña 48/19; 63/9
cañón 45/6, 14
caparazón 59/5
capitán 44/5
capó 38/26
capricornio 5/5
cápsula 4/19; 63/4
capulla 59/28; 62/25
cara 9/C
caracol 58/13
carámbano 27/8
cárcel 16/B
carga 42/6
cargador 54/6
Caribe 6/18
carlinga 45/22
carne 20/13
carnicero 54/2
carpeta 21/18
carpintero 54/3
carrera 46/A
carreta 40/26
carrete 53/8; 73/9
carretera 15/34; 38/18; 39/2
carretilla 14/4; 27/27
carretón 42/17
carril 39/5, 6
cartel 18/24
cartera 18/9; 67/3, 16
cartero 22/5
casa 26; 37/3
cascada 34/4
casco 16/2; 17/2, 40/27
caseta 41/23
caspio 6/24
castillo 35/23, 52/4
cavar 64/10
cayado 36/27
cazuela 30/12
cebo 48/22
cebolla 62/13
cebra 57/24
cedro 63/23
ceja 9/8, 16
celda 16/15
cemento 23/16
cenicero 51/10
ceniza 51/9
centígrado 70/C
centímetro 80
central 37/6
centralita 21/15
centro 68/20
cepillo 25/2, 30/27; 31/6, 10,

32/18, 20; 33/15, 18
cercado 76/15
cerdo 56/3
cerebro 9/21
cereza 61/7
cerilla 51/6
cero 80
cerrar 65/13
cerrojo 28/7, 8
césped 27/19
cesta 20/7; 30/23; 46/15;
  67/10
cesto 33/26; 40/34
cien 80
ciempiés 58/22
cigarrillo 51/8
cilindro 68/25
cima 34/3
címbalo 49/29
cimiento 23/11
cincel 24/4
cinco 80
cincuenta 80
cinta 53
cintura 8/16
cinturón 13/10; 38/24
círculo 5/2, 6, 68/E
circumferencia 68/18
ciruela 61/23
cisne 60/17
ciudad 14
clarinete 49/2
claro 75/11
clavícula 8/2
clavo 25/11
cliente 20/5; 51/22
cobertizo 26/20; 27/26
cobrador 15/27
cocina 30; 30/1
coco 61/9
cocodrilo 59/1
coche 15/33; 16/5, 17/7;
  39/16; 41/3
cochecito 14/18
codo 8/23
cofre 38/2
cogedor 31/8
coger 66/8
cohete 4/16
cojín 29/9
col 62/11
cola 56/23; 58/7
colador 30/25
colcha 32/7
colchón 32/8
colegio 18
colibrí 60/27
coliflor 62/10
colina 34/10
colmena 36/25
colmillo 57/23
color 79
collar 12/11
coma 69/21
combinación 12/2
combustible 37/9
comer 64/17
cometa 4/1; 35/30
comisaría 16/4
cómoda 32/15
compartimiento 41/4
compás 18/11
concha 35/27; 58/14
conducir 64/15
conductor 41/2; 54/12
conejo 56/20
congelador 20/14
Congo 7/50
cono 68/23
constelación 4/2
construcción 23
consultorio 17/13
contador 19/4
continente 6/A
contra 73/8
contrabajo 49/9
Coral 6/29
corazón 52/13, 61/4
corbata 11/4
corcho 51/25
cordero 36/30
Cordillera 7/D
cordón 11/9; 28/28

cortar 64/8; 66/23
corte 15/C
corteza 63/17
cortina 26/14; 29/7; 50/6
corto 74/16
corral 36/5
correa 11/22
corredor 47/28
correo 22/7, 10
Correos 22
correr 65/9
cosechadora 36/16
coser 65/11
costa 5/11
costilla 8/5
costura 53; 53/3
costurera 54/10
coupé 38/39
craneo 8/1
creciente 4/11
crema 12/18
cremallera 53/22
cresta 60 /12
cricket 48/B
cristal 19/17
cruce 14/16
cuadernillo 18/18
cuadrado 68/C
cuadrante 19/5
cuadrilla 72/7
cuadro 29/12
cuál 79/E
cuarenta 80
cuarto 4/14; 33, 69/14, 70/7,
  73/4; 80
cuatro 80
cubierta 43/19; 52/16
cubo 30/9; 31/19; 35/24; 67/8,
  68/24
cucaracha 59/14
cuchara 29/37
cucharita 17/31
cucharón 23/24
cuchillo 24/5; 29/28, 41
cuello 8/11; 11/2
cuerda 22/21; 27/28; 46/14,
  49/5; 73/5
cuerno 56/9; 57/26
cuerpo 8
cuervo 60/33
culata 38/36
cumbre 34/3
cuna 32/26
cuneta 14/10
cuñada 71/8
cuñado 71/8
curva 68/3

CH
chal 13/5
chaleco 11/5
chalet 35/8
chaqueta 10/8
chica 12, 13
chico 10, 11
chimenea 26/2; 29/4, 37/7;
  42/9; 43/21
China 7/31, 32
chocolate 73/2
chupete 32/28

D
dama 52/9
Danubio 7/47
dar 65/22, 66/3, 10, 11
dátil 61/10
debajo 76/3
débil 75/6
décimo 80
decorados 50/4
dedal 53/5
dedo 8/30, 9/41
defendido 16; 20
defensa 45, 47/15, 16
delante 47/20–24; 76/7
delantero 42/22
delfín 57/3
delgado 75/15
delta 5/9
dentista 17/16
dentro 76/10
dependiente 20/8

deporte 46–48
depósito 57/14
derecho 74/5
desaguadero 30/8
desague 33/5
descapotable 38/38
desordenado 75/7
despensa 30/6
destornillador 24/7
detención 16/A
detrás 76/16
día 80
diagonal 68/15
diámetro 68/19
diapositivo 52/30
diario 21/5
dibujar 64/12
diciembre 80
diecinueve 80
dieciocho 80
dieciséis 80
diecisiete 80
diente 9/12
diez 80
difícil 74/12
dirección 22/11
disco 28/27; 29/20
disparar 65/12
dividido 69/18
dobladilla 53/4
doctor 17/21; 55/8
domingo 80
dormir 66/19
dormitorio 32
dos 80
ducha 33/4
duro 74/13

E
eclipse 4/10
Ecuador 5/4
Educación 18
ejército 45/A
él 79
eléctrica 37
electricista 58/2
elefante 57/21
ella 79
embalse 37/1
embarcación 43/26
embrague 38/20
empeine 9/39
empleado 54/4
empujar 55/6
empuñadura 33/8
en 76
encaje 53/9
encendido 38/14
encima 77/1
enchufe 31/15
energía 37
enero 80
enfermera 55/10
enjambre 72/16
entre 79/12
equipo 72/15
equipaje 44/4
erizo 56/26
escalera 17/8; 23/5; 28/17
escalón 23/6
escama 58/9
escaparate 15/23; 20/1
escarabajo 59/13
escena 50/1
escoba 31/2
escorpión 58/27
escribir 66/2, 21
escritorio 21/1
escuadra 18/16
escuchar 65/1
esencia 12/16
esfera 70/4
esmalte 12/15
espalda 8/15
espantapájaros 36/13
espejo 36/12
espiga 63/2
espina 8/6
espiral 59/7; 68/1
esponja 33/24
esposa 16/8; 71/1
espuma 35/32

esquí 47/26
esquiador 47/25
esquina 69/3
estación 39/7; 41/13
estacionamiento 15/32
estadio 47/B
estanque 34/19; 36/9
estante 30/16
estantería 20/15; 30/10; 50/25
este 5/C; 79
estera 33/23
esternón 8/4
estetoscopio 17/22
estómago 8/17
estrado 18/6
estrangulador 38/15
estrecho 75/1
estrella 4/5
estribo 46/6
estuario 5/10
etiqueta 22/22
Europa 6/3
excavadora 23/20
excavar 64/10
expediente 21/18
extinctor 17/6
extremo 47/20, 24

F
fácil 74/12
faisán 60/14
falda 13/2
familiar 71
faro 38/29; 40/5
fase 4/B
febrero 80
fecha 70
feliz 74/11
felpudo 26/18
feo 75/9
fila 72/14
flamenco 60/8
flauta 49/1
flor 27/20; 62
florero 29/14
florista 55/5
flota 72/4
foco 50/7
forma 68
foso 50/12
foto 52/22
fotografía 52/D, 22
fotógrafo 55/4
fracción 69/22
frasco 17/30; 19/16
fregasuelos 31/5
freno 38/19, 22; 40/14
frente 9/8; 69/7
fresa 17/17; 61/21
frío 74/15
fronda 61/33
fruncir 66/14
fruta 20/17; 61
fuego 29/6
fuente 73/14
fuera 76/1, 11; 77/6
fuerte 75/6
furgoneta 38/40
fuselaje 44/10
fusil 45/2
fútbol 47/A

G
gafa 11/23, 40/28
gajo 61/17
galaxia 4/3
galería 50/9
gallina 36/33
gancho 53/23
Ganges 7/52
ganso 60/25
garage 26/6
garganta 8/12
garra 60/3
garza 60/15
gasolinera 39/7
gatillo 45/13
gatito 56/16
gato 56/15
gaviota 60/12
girar 66/10, 16

girasol 62/27
globo 5/A; 9/15
glorieta 39/4
Gobi 7/44
gol 46/25; 47/7
golfo 6/C
golondrina 60/22
golpear 66/5
goma 18/14
gorra 10/16; 13/4
gorrión 60/28
gorro 46/9
gota 27/4
grado 70/C
gramo 80
granja 36; 36/7
granjero 36/15
grano 63/5
grapa 21/8
grapadora 21/7
grifo 33/2, 3
grillo 59/11
gris 79
grúa 23/1; 42/4
grueso 74/10; 75/15
grupo 72/11
guante 11/20; 33/17; 46/12; 48/3
guardabarros 40/10
guardameta 47/14
guardapolvos 52/17
guardián 16/13
guía 28/29
Guinea 6/19
guisante 62/3
guitarra 49/26

H
habichuela 62/1
hacia 77/10
hacha 24/15; 25/7
halcón 60/6
hamaca 35/19
hangar 44/21
hebilla 13/11
helado 35/17
helecho 61/32
hélice 43/14; 44/18
helicóptero 44/15
henil 36/1
heno 36/2
hermoso 75/9
herramientas 25
hervir 66/22
hibisco 62/24
hierba 26/21
hígado 9/25
higo 61/29
hija 71/3
hijo 71/3
hilo 48/20
Himalaya 7/40
hipopótamo 57/20
hipotenusa 68/12
hobbies 52
hocico 56/4
hockey 46/D
hogar 31
hoja 21/10; 27/15; 63/15
hombre 10, 11
hombro 8/13
hora 70
horario 18/22; 41/15
horizonte 42/1
hormiga 59/17
hormigón 23/25
hornillo 19/12
horno 30/2
horquilla 24/10; 27/25
hotel 35/7
Hudson 6/16
hueco 75/14
huella 16/11, 12
hueso 61/8, 20
huevo 20/11

I
iguala 69/19
imán 19/19
imperdible 53/10
impermeable 11/12

indicador 38/5, 13
índice 50/24
Índico 6/13
Indus 7/31
instalación 37/10
interior 47/21, 23
interruptor 31/17
intestino 9/27
inyector 17/4
iris 9/20

J
jabón 33/25
Japón 7/33
jardín 27
jardinera 26/13
jardinero 55/3
jarra 19/15; 30/20; 51/3
jarrita 29/37
jarro 51/14
jaula 67/14
jeep 45/5
jefe 41/10
jersey 10/6; 13/5
jinete 46/1
jirafa 57/15
joroba 56/7
joven 75/2
joyero 32/23
juego 52/1
jueves 80
juez 16/22; 47/2
jugador 46/24
julio 80
junco 43/5
junio 80
junto 76/14, 15
jurado 16/17

K
Kalahari 7/42

L
labio 9/13
lacre 22/19
lado 68/13; 69/5
ladrillo 23/8
lagarta 59/9
lago 5/13; 34/5
lamer 64/25
lámpara 29/15; 32/25
lana 53/19
lancha 43/12
langosta 58/12; 59/10
lápiz 12/19; 18/15
largo 74/16
lata 30/19, 22; 51/4
látigo 40/25
latitud 5/15
lavabo 33/11
lavado 27/29
lavar 65/25
leche 20/10
lechuga 62/12
leer 65/7
lengua 9/14; 59/8
lente 19/10
lento 74/9
león 57/16
leopardo 57/18
Ley 16
libélula 59/19
librería 29/10
libro 18/19; 52/15
ligero 75/12
lima 12/12; 24/2
limón 61/14
limpiaparabrisas 38/11
limpio 74/3
Línea 68; 41/24; 47/8, 12, 13; 48/26
linterna 16/9
líquido 30/28
litro 80
lobo 57/11
locomotora 41/3
locutor 54/15
lomo 52/18
longitud 5/14; 69/11
loro 60/20

luchador 46/22
luchar 64/19
lugar 79
Luna 4/5
lunes 80
lupa 16/10
luz 17/18; 28/22; 38/4; 40/30
lychee 61/26

LL
llama 17/15; 56/5
llana 23/17
llanura 34/1
llave 24/6, 13; 28/15
lleno 74/8
llevar 64/3
llorar 64/7
lluvia 27/3

M
maceta 27/24
macizo 27/21; 75/14
madre 71/4
maíz 63/11
malecón 42/2
malo 75/8
mandíbula 9/9
manga 11/7
mango 25/16; 61/15
manguera 17/3
manilla 70/A
manillar 40/6
mano 8/27
manojo 72/2
manta 32/6
mantel 51/30
mantequera 29/32
mantilla 12/5
mantis 59/15
manzana 61/1
mapa 5/B; 18/21
máquina 21/21; 31/4; 33/12
mar 35; 6
marco 26/9; 29/13
margarita 62/18
marido 71/1
marina 45/B
marinero 55/15
mariposa 59/25
marrón 79
martes 80
martín 60/30
marzo 80
más 69/15
máscara 48/3
mástil 43/3
matasellos 22/8
matrícula 38/28
mazo 19/20; 25/1
mecánico 54/5
mecanógrafa 54/9
media 4/12; 12/4
médico 17
medida 69
medio 47/17-19
Mediterráneo 6/22
medusa 58/11
Méjico 6/17
mejilla 9/5
Mekong 7/53
melena 57/17
melocotón 61/19
mellado 74/2
menguante 4/14
menos 69/17
menú 51/23
meridional 6/14
mes 80
mesa 29/19, 23
mesilla 32/9
metro 80
mezcladora 23/21
microbús 38/40
micrófono 49/25
microscopio 19/9
miércoles 80
mil 80
mililitro 80
milímetro 80
millón 80
minero 54/7
minutero 70/A

minuto 80
mío 79
mirlo 60/32
misil 45/6
Misisipí 7/45
mochila 35/4
molinete 42/16
mondadura 61/18
moneda 20/25
mono 57/12
montaña 7/36; 34/2
mortero 19/21
mosca 59/23
mosquito 59/20
mostacero 51/28
mostrador 20/4, 22; 22/3; 50/25
motocicleta 14/17; 39/20
motor 38/31; 44/12
motora 35/34
moza 51/17
mozo 54/14
muchedumbre 72/3
muelle 42/5
muleta 17/26
multiplicado 69/16
mundo 5
muñeca 8/25; 32/31
muñeco 27/7
músculo 9/31
músico 49/3
muslo 8/33

N
nadador 35/35
nadar 65/20
nalga 8/19
naranja 61/16; 79
nariz 9/2
navegar 65/10
neceser 67/18
Negro 6/23; 79
nénufar 62/26
neumático 40/11
nido 60/29
nieta 71/12
nieto 71/12
Níger 7/49
Nilo 7/48
nombre 72
noroeste 5/C
Norte 5/1; 5/C; 6/20
noveno 80
noventa 80
noviembre 80
nuero 71/7
nuestro 79
nueve 80
número 80; 41/21

O
objeto 31
obra 23
obtuso 68/10
octavo 80
ochenta 80
ocho 80
oeste 5/C
oficial 22/1
oficina 21
oficio 54
ojal 53/16
ojo 9/1; 28/6
ola 35/33
oleoducto 37/12
omóplato 8/3
once 80
operario 39/10; 50/16
órbita 4/9
oreja 9/3
órgano 9/E
orinal 32/32
oscuro 75/11
osito 32/29
oso 57/8
ostra 58/16
ovalo 68/F
oveja 36/29
ovillo 73/1

P

paciente 17/20
pacífico 6/1, 10
padre 71/4
página 52/9
paja 51/12
pajar 36/4
pala 23/13; 24/9; 35/25; 46/19
palanca 38/21; 40/38
paleta 13/26; 24/12; 30/31;
  35/21; 43/9
palma 8/28
palmera 63/19
palmípedo 60/9
paloma 60/24
pan 20/19
panadero 55/7
panel 45/28
pantalla 29/18; 50/18; 52/27
pantalon 10/7, 12; 11/17;
  13/6; 46/8
pantorrilla 8/35
pañal 32/36
paño 30/29
pañuelo 13/13, 14; 32/22
papaya 61/25
papel 21/20; 23/12; 33/9
papelera 15/20; 21/13
paquete 22/20; 73/11
parabrisas 38/10
paracaídas 45/25
parachoques 38/6; 41/29
parada 15/28
paraguas 11/24; 13/17
pared 26/3; 29/2
parentesco 71
párpado 9/17
parque 14/12
parquímetro 15/25
partitura 49/12
parrilla 30/3
pasador 40/19
pasajero 44/6
pasamanos 28/19
pasaporte 44/3
pasarela 47/10
pasar 66/13
pasillo 50/21
paso 39/2
pasta 33/19
pastor 36/26
patata 66/2
patín 47/31
patinador 47/32
patio 26/5; 36/6
patito 36/31
pato 36/32
patrón 53/20
pavo 60/11, 16
payaso 54/13
pecho 8/14
pedal 40/17; 49/17
pegamento 18/13
peinar 66/12
peine 32/21
pelo 8/9
pelota 35/26; 46/17
peluca 16/25
peluquero 54/1
pelvis 8/7
penalty 47/10, 11
pendiente 12/10
pepino 62/8
pera 61/22
percha 28/14; 32/19
perchero 28/13
perforadora 21/6
perfume 12/16
periquito 60/26
periscopio 45/20
perno 25/8
persiana 26/15
pérsico 6/26
perrezno 56/14
perro 36/28; 56/13
pesa 14/3
pesado 75/12
pesca 48/C
pescador 48/18
peso 80
pestaña 9/18
pestañiña 12/14

pétalo 62/20
pez 58
piano 49/15
pico 23/12; 60/4, 19
pichón 60/35
pie 8/37
piel 61/3; 6, 18
pierna 8/32
pijama 10/4; 32/27
pila 30/7
piloto 45/27
pimentero 51/29
pincel 18/25
pingüino 60/13
pintura 13/27
pinza 27/30; 58/18
piña 61/24; 63/21
pipeta 19/18
pirámide 68/22
pista 44/19; 48/23
pistola 45/10
pita 42/14
pito 47/4
pitorro 29/34
pizarra 18/2
placa 30/4
plancha 31/11
planchar 66/18
planeador 44/14
planeta 4/4
planicie 34/1
planta 61; 9/41
plataforma 4/17; 49/13
plátano 61/5
platillo 19/2; 29/31
plato 72/13
playa 35/11
pliegue 53/11
pluma 18/17; 60/5
policía 16/1; 55/13
polilla 59/26
polo 5/1, 7
polvera 12/13
polvo 31/9, 18
pollito 36/35
pollo 36/33
ponerse 65/17
pop 49/B
por ciento 69/20
porra 16/7
portaobjetos 19/11
portaviones 45/18
portero 47/12
posesivo 79
poste 14/B; 15/24; 43/11
potrillo 56/2
prado 34/11
preposición 76
presa 37/2
primero 80
primo 71/9
prisión 16/B
prisionero 16/14
proa 4/15
profesión 54
profesora 18/1
profundidad 69/10
profundo 74/6
pronombre 79
proyector 50/15; 52/29
pueblo 34/16
puente 14/13
puerco 56/26
puerta 26/7; 27/16
puesto 14/3
pulgar 8/29
pulmón 9/24
pulpo 58/23
pulsera 12/9
puntada 53/17
punto 53/21
puño 11/3
pupila 9/19
pupitre 18/7
púrpura 79

Q

queso 20/9

R

rabo 61/2, 62/2

radiador 38/33
radio 29/22; 38/25, 40/12;
  68/17
radiografía 17/24
raíz 63/11
rama 63/13
ramita 27/14; 63/14
ramo 72/1
rana 58/20
raqueta 48/27
rascador 30/26
rasgar 65/21
rata 56/22
ratón 56/18
rebanada 73/8
rebaño 72/6, 10
rebeca 10/13
receptor 48/1
recibo 20/23
recipiente 67
recreo 46
red 46/20; 48/24
refinería 37/13
regadera 27/23
regla 18/10, 20
reina 52/7, 12
reir 64/24
rejilla 38/27; 41/9
reloj 11/21; 28/24; 32/24
remo 43/7
remolacha 62/9
remolcador 42/19
remolque 39/13, 21
reno 56/11
repisa 29/5
repollo 62/11
réptil 59/A
restaurante 51
retrete 33/7
retrovisor 38/1
revólver 45/12
rey 52/8, 13
rienda 40/24; 46/4
ring 46/13
rinocerante 57/25
riñón 9/26
río 7/F; 34/12
roble 63/10
roca 35/29
rodilla 8/34
rojo 6/25; 79
rollo 52/24; 73/12
rompeolas 35/10
romper 64/2, 65/21
rompevientos 35/18
ropa 10; 32/17
rosa 62/19; 79
rosca 25/10
rotor 44/16
rueda 40/9; 58/15
ruidoso 75/13

S

sábado 80
sábana 32/5
sacacorchos 51/11
saca 22/6
saco 35/3; 67/13
Sáhara 7/41
sala 29; 41/18; 44/1; 50/14
salchicha 20/12
salero 51/27
salida 17/10
salmón 58/4
saltar 64/21
sandalia 13/7
sarta 72/8
satélite 4/18
sauce 63/24
saxofón 49/22
secador 31/14
seco 74/7
secretaria 21/22
sector 68/21
segundero 70/A
segundo 80
seis 80
seiscientos 80
sello 22/9, 18
selva 34/9
semáforo 14/7
semilla 62/28

senda 27/18
sentarse 65/15
seña 22/11
septiembre 80
séptimo 80
serpentear 64/6
serpiente 59/6
serrucho 25/17
sesenta 80
seta 62/14
setenta 80
seto 27/17; 34/14
sexto 80
sien 9/7
sierra 25/18
siete 80
silla 17/15; 46/3
sillín 40/7
snorkel 35/16
sobaco 8/20
sobre 21/11; 22/14
sobrina 71/11
sobrino 71/11
sofá 29/21
Sol 4/8; 27/9
solapa 11/15; 22/15
soldado 45/1
sollozar 64/7
sombra 12/17
sombrero 11/13
sombrilla 35/12
sonajero 32/30
sonreir 65/16
soñar 64/14
soplar 64/1
sostén 12/1
sota 52/11
su 79
suave 75/5
subir 64/5
submarino 45/19
sucio 74/3
suegra 71/6
suegro 71/6
suela 11/10
suelo 28/11
suelto 75/16
suéter 13/5
sujetapapeles 21/9
sumadora 21/3
supermercado 20
sur 5/C; 7/31
sureste 5/C
suroeste 5/C
suyo 79

T
tablero 38/12; 46/16; 53/2
tableta 73/3
tablón 23/11
taburete 19/8; 32/11; 49/18;
   51/20
tacón 11/11
taladradora 25/3, 4
taladro 23/23
talón 9/38
taller 24
tallo 62/23
tambor 49/30
tamiz 30/30
tanque 45/8
tapacubos 38/30
tapón 33/6; 38/3; 51/2
taquilla 41/14
tarjeta 22/13
Tasmania 6/30
taxi 14/5
taza 29/30
té 63/8
teatro 50/A
techo 29/1
tejado 26/1
tejido 53/13
tela 35/2; 53/13
telaraña 58/26
teléfono 21/2; 28/25
telegrama 22/16
televisión 29/17
temperatura 70
tenaza 24/14; 58/18
tener 66/20
tentáculo 58/24

tercio 69/13
termómetro 17/28; 70/C
termos 67/9
ternera 36/22
terrón 75/7
testigo 16/19
tetera 29/36
tetilla 32/34
texto 52/21
ti 79
tía 71/10
tiburón 58/1
tiempo 27
tienda 22/15; 35/1
Tierra 4/7
tijera 24/11; 53/26
timbre 28/3; 40/2
timón 44/13
tío 71/10
tirar 65/5

tiza 18/4
toalla 30/32; 33/20; 35/14
toallera 33/21
tobillo 8/36
tocadiscos 29/11; 51/15
tocador 32/10
tocar 65/22
toga 16/24
tomacorrientes 31/16
tomate 62/15
torcido 74/5
tormenta 27/2
tornillo 25/9
torno 24/8
toro 36/23
torpedo 45/17
tortuga 59/24
torre 37/5, 8, 11; 44/20
trabajador 23/14
tractor 36/18
trainera 43/17
traje 4/21; 11/6; 35/36; 46/23
tramo 72/5
tranquilo 75/4
transatlántico 43/20
transbordador 43/15
transportadora 18/12; 39/12
trapo 31/7
tráquea 9/22
trasero 8/19
traviesas 41/25
treinta 80
tren 41/1
trepar 64/5
triángulo 68/13
tribuna 47/5
trigo 36/14
trineo 47/29
trípode 19/13; 52/28
triste 74/11
trombón 49/20
trompa 49/18; 57/22
trompeta 49/19
tronco 27/12; 53/18
Trópico 5/35
trozo 73/7, 8
trueno 27/2
tubería 19/14; 23/9
tubo 19/22; 38/7; 40/35
tuerco 25/13
tulipán 62/22

U
Ujotsk 7/34
último 75/10
umbral 28/4
universo 4
uno 80
uña 8/31
Urales 7/39
uva 61/12

V
vaca 36/21
vacío 74/8
vagón 41/28
vaina 62/4
válvula 40/13
valla 36/10
valle 34/6
vara 49/21

vaso 29/29; 33/16; 51/26
veinte 80
veintiuno 80
véjiga 9/28
vela 43/4
velocímetro 38/16
vena 9/29
vendaje 17/27
ventana 26/8
ventilador 21/14
verbo 64, 65
verde 79
vergel 36/12
vértice 68/8
vestido 13/8
viaje 38; 4/C
vidrio 26/10
viernes 80
vigésimo 80
viña 61/13
viola 49/7
violín 49/4
violoncello 49/8
volante 38/17; 53/14
volar 64/20
volquete 23/22
vuelta 11/18
vuestra 79

Y
yacer 65/3
Yangtse 7/55
yate 43/1
yerno 71/7

Z
zanahoria 62/5
zapatilla 10/5; 12/7
zapato 10/9; 15; 11/8
zigzag 78/6
zona 47/10, 11
zorra 56/24